Get Everything Done

And Still Have Time to Play

Mark Forster

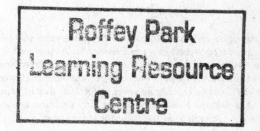
Hodder & Stoughton
LONDON SYDNEY AUCKLAND

The Scripture quotations contained herein are from the New Revised Standard
Version Bible, copyright © 1989 by the Division of Christian Education of the
National Council of the Churches of Christ in the USA. Used by permission.
All rights reserved.

Translations from Dante's *Divine Comedy* are the author's own.

British Library Cataloguing in Publication Data
A record for this book is available from the British Library

ISBN 0 340 74620 3

Typeset by Avon Dataset Ltd, Bidford-on-Avon, Warks

Printed and bound in Great Britain by
The Guernsey Press Co. Ltd, Channel Isles

Hodder & Stoughton
A Division of Hodder Headline Ltd
338 Euston Road
London NW1 3BH

To Lucy

Contents

Acknowledgments

I want to thank my clients and the wonderful community of life coaches in the United Kingdom, to whom I owe more than I can possibly say. Out of the many who have given me their help and support I would like to single out Sarah Litvinoff, without whom this book would never have existed, and George Metcalfe for his unwavering encouragement.

Introduction

The title of this book, *Get Everything Done – And Still Have Time to Play*, may sound like an impossible dream to many of us, as we struggle with the ever-increasing busyness of the modern world. Today's technology and communications have ensured that more and more strident voices are laying claim to our attention. Profound changes in the workplace and in the structures of society seem to have had the undesired and unintended effect of increasing the pressure both to perform and to 'have it all'. Work and play have become sharply divided in our minds, as if they were in a life-or-death struggle to increase their share of our lives. We act as if every minute spent on play was crippling our work and every minute spent on work was taking time from our 'real' lives of fun, family and friends.

It is my deep conviction that this apparent competition between work and play is not the true picture. I believe the reality is that if we do not find time to play our work suffers, and correspondingly our personal lives are enriched by work well done. I believe

1

too that working in a concentrated and purposeful way is less stressful than working in a distracted or unfocused way, and that we can do more and better work when we deliberately limit our working hours. Even as I write this introduction I have been reading in the papers that the French law limiting working hours to a maximum of thirty-five hours per week has had the effect of increasing French industry's competitiveness, instead of reducing it as was widely expected when it was introduced.

In short I believe that when work and play are in balance, they contribute to each other. More than that, work is done best when it is seen as a form of play, and play benefits from being taken as seriously as we take our work. It is my hope and belief that this book will enable you to bring your life into this balance. But reading it on its own will not do the trick; you must take action to put what it contains into practice, and in particular work through the many exercises it contains.

Before we even get into the body of the book I want to give you an exercise which is intended to be a continuing daily practice both while you are working through this book and thereafter. Although I think there is an important place for quick-fix techniques – I shall be giving you plenty in this book – getting control of our lives is essentially a matter of training and persistence. This exercise will go a long way towards achieving this for you. Done properly it is both immensely effective and great fun.

Exercise: Mental strength training

Are you strong-minded? Can you do anything you set your mind to without fail? Or are you a mental weakling who never succeeds in doing half the things you intend to – who spends your time reacting to circumstances instead of progressing your aims and ambitions? The very fact that you are reading this book at all means that you probably feel that your mental strength leaves something to be desired.

Strength of mind used to be considered one of the most important qualities that a person could have. These days it gets much less attention than either intelligence or education, but that does not change the fact that it is probably even more important for a successful and happy life. This is an exercise to develop your mental strength, just as weight-training can develop your physical strength. It uses principles similar to those used in weight-training, increasing both the resistance and the number of repetitions according to capacity. Like a progressive weight-training programme, it is always tailored to exactly the amount of strength that you have at the time.

All you have to do is every evening decide on one thing you are going to do the next day without fail. Pitch its level of difficulty so that it is easy enough for you to be reasonably confident of being able to do it. Then the following day do it!

If you successfully complete your task, then decide on another one for the following day and make it just a little bit more difficult. But you still need to be pretty confident that you are going to be able to do it.

If you don't succeed in doing it, then you have pitched your task so it is too hard for you. Don't accept any excuses from yourself for not doing your task. If you haven't done it, then you have failed – period. So make the next day's task easier, enough for you to be absolutely certain of being able to do it. Continue each day, making the next day's task a little harder each time you are successful and a little easier each time you fail. Gradually stretch yourself further and further, falling back only when you overreach yourself. Make sure you define your task clearly each day, so you know whether you have achieved it or not.

This exercise is surprisingly difficult for some people. They are so used to reacting to what is going on around them and acting on impulse that the idea of doing something because they have made a prior conscious decision to do it is contrary to their whole way of thinking. You are probably not in anything like as bad a position as this, but nevertheless it is best when starting to choose tasks that you feel are really easy for you to do. You can then quickly increase the difficulty until you are pushing against your maximum capacity. It doesn't matter whether these tasks are to do with work or leisure. For that matter they can even be completely pointless. What counts is that you do them for no other reason than that you have *decided* to do them.

Eventually you will work your way up to being able to decide to do one really difficult task each day and do it every time. When you have got to this point you are ready to move on to the next phase. This is to select *two* items each day. Drop the level of difficulty so that you are confident of being able to complete both tasks. Work your way up to maximum difficulty again and then start on three tasks a day. Continue this way until you arrive at the point where you can list everything you are going to do the following day and know for sure that you will do the lot without fail. What sort of effect do you think that might have on your life? Take a moment to list some of the ways your life would be different.

It may take you a long time to reach this point, quite possibly years – but persevere one day at a time. The effect is progressive as in weight-training. But even at the early stages you will find it is making a noticeable difference to the amount of control you have over your life. It shares another characteristic with weight-training: reading about it will make no difference at all. The exercise will only increase your strength if you do it. In the meantime, you have the rest of this book to help you on your way!

Part One

Managing Your Time – Or Managing Your Life?

Nel mezzo del cammin di nostra vita
Mi ritrovai per una selva oscura,
Che la diritta via era smarrita.

Halfway through the journey of our life
I found that I was wandering in a dark wood
And realised that I'd lost the straight way.

(Dante, *Inferno*, I, 1–3)

1

My Own Experience

If you have a problem with getting things done, you are not alone. The world is full of people like us. Like us? – yes, because I have had just as much a problem in the past as anyone else. But there is hope for all who suffer from this. What I intend to share with you in this chapter is my own experience of changing myself from someone with little control over his life to someone who – most of the time anyway – can get everything done and still find time to play. In fact my life is now so varied and interesting that I regard most of what I do as play. The greatest change that has happened to me is that I have learned to enjoy my life now, today, not some time in the future when things will be different. Here's the story of how I did it.

I have had a problem with time all my life

Too many books about managing time seem to be written by people who sound as if they have never had a problem with organising themselves. Most of their advice is pitched at too high a level for those of us who are struggling, and only succeeds in making us feel guilty because we can't live up to what they are expecting us to do. This book is different – it is written by someone who is naturally disorganised. All my life I have struggled with time, and suffered the agonies of frustration which are caused by procrastination and lack of order. So if you find fitting everything into the day impossible, then I understand fully what it feels like from my own painful experience.

In this book I will be sharing with you my own history of struggling to get organised and how in desperation I started to develop my own techniques. I will be sharing these techniques with you, knowing that they have already helped many people. And during my journey, I discovered that there is no such thing as managing time – time just is. What we can learn to manage is how, when and where we direct our attention. I will be returning many times in these pages to the theme that regular focused attention is the key to virtually every problem and challenge in life, and the more we learn how to direct and focus our attention the more skilled we will be at life. This is because anything that we give our attention to will start to change. Of course everything changes constantly anyway, whatever we do. But the choice we have is whether to be involved in the change or not. If we leave the washing up undone for days, it will change so it becomes hard, congealed and repellent. If we pay attention to it, it will change in a different way – so it becomes clean, tidy and reusable. Human attention is the way humanity has progressed, and when humanity has failed to progress it has usually been because we have resisted or ignored change instead of paying attention to it.

This is not, however, intended to be a work of philosophy but a purely practical manual, written for the disorganised whatever their circumstances. But as you put the techniques contained in it into effect, you will gain more control over your life and discover a new sense of power, the sense that if you set out to achieve something it won't be you that lets yourself down. The fear of failure will diminish because you know you can at last trust yourself to carry something through.

Some of my earliest memories are about procrastination. As a schoolboy I used to put off homework until the very last moment. It was amazing how good I was at not doing it. I would prefer finishing an essay by getting up at 5 a.m. on a freezing cold morning (those were the days before central heating and insulation were commonplace), rather than do it in relative comfort the evening before. In fact it was because the evening was so comfortable that I didn't want to spoil it with homework. But inevitably there were mornings when I failed to get up and then I had to suffer the consequences of late homework (and in those days there were quite considerable consequences to suffer).

If procrastination is a problem during our schooldays, it becomes much worse once we become adults and start work at a job. School and university have a fairly clear structure to them. At any one time there are only a relatively few things you are supposed to be doing. But the adult world and adult responsibilities are different. Unless your job is of the simplest repetitive kind there is a huge increase in the number of things you could be doing. In any sort of managerial or executive position this multiplies again, and if you run your own business there is a virtually infinite number of possibilities. The result of this is that it becomes only too easy to be very busy without actually achieving much. We get taken over by trivia – usually because trivia represent the path of least resistance.

My work was always severely hampered by not being able to do things when they would best have been done. I struggled with tasks, only to find that I would do almost anything to avoid doing them. And the more I put them off, the more difficult they became to do.

I was good at my work when I did it. But procrastination made me unreliable and therefore reduced my chances of advancement.

It was not through lack of intelligence or ability that I failed to reach my potential, but simply the crippling effects of bad time-management and procrastination.

It was not just my paid work that the problem affected. I had many schemes for self-betterment and for making money, which I would rush into but fail to finish. Once the initial enthusiasm wore off, resistance built up and I found I was unable to follow them through.

So procrastination became a way of life for me. A way of life that severely damaged my quality of life. I always felt I was missing out on much of what life had to offer – simply because I never got around to making it better.

I found some people were naturally good at managing their lives

Most people I knew and worked with seemed to have much the same sort of problem as I did to a greater or lesser extent. With different people the problem manifested itself in different ways. Some would be better at seeing projects through but worse at timekeeping. Some would have no problem with things they enjoyed doing but were hopeless at anything else. Some were completely unreliable at routine work but could dream up and carry through the most amazing creative projects. But hardly anyone I knew seemed to be living life at their full capacity, certainly not in all aspects of their life.

I had the good fortune to work for two people who were exceptions to this rule. They were very different in character but they shared the common trait that they were always on top of their work. They had highly responsible positions in a very difficult and dangerous situation. They spent as little time as possible at their desks, preferring to be out in the field, yet their desks were always not just tidy but completely clear. However much paperwork came their way, it never stayed on their desks. Everything was actioned immediately; there was no hanging around for decisions to be made. The result was that the business in hand went forward quickly, and there was never any sense that they were merely reacting to circumstances.

Of course much of this was done by delegation, and I was one of those to whom much of the routine work was delegated. But I knew only too well that if I had been in their position my desk would have been weighed down with paper, I would have been immersed in trivia and important decisions would never have been made.

On a much smaller scale, my wife has the same ability to do what needs doing when it needs doing. I have always admired the way in which she can organise complicated events using little more than a shopping list. Even more totally mysterious to me is her habit of starting her Christmas shopping for the following Christmas at the January sales – my Christmas shopping has always been done on Christmas Eve.

So it can be done – both by people in high pressure, high responsibility jobs and by those simply living an ordinary everyday life with all its ups and downs. When people are working effectively like this, unnecessary stress is eliminated. They are much more able to focus on the big picture and that helps the decision-making process. A characteristic of people who manage their time well is that they are decisive but not impulsive.

Natural time-managers achieve this with the aid of very few techniques. I never saw either of my two bosses use a to-do list. They just seemed to know what needed to be done and to do it. My wife makes shopping lists and present lists but not to-do lists.

I will be exploring later in this book how we can achieve the state of mind in which we do what needs to be done when it needs to be done, without the aid of lists or techniques. But for most of us it does not come naturally. We cannot run before we can walk. We need techniques to train us. If one day we can cast these crutches aside that is all to the good. We need a 'system' to lift us out of our difficulties, but we do not want to become prisoners of that system. There are more important things in life than living mechanically or automatically. So let us start by looking at some of the differences between the ways that good time-managers and poor time-managers act, in the belief that, if we can alter our behaviour in the direction of the good time-managers, many of our problems with time will disappear.

People who are successful at managing their lives work in a very different way from those who aren't

From my observation of the people I have mentioned above and many others, I have learnt that people who manage their time successfully (and that means people who manage their *lives* successfully) share certain characteristics which bad time-managers do not have. Of course each individual case is not as cut and dried as I am going to present it, but nevertheless there are consistent ways of acting that characterise the naturally good time-manager.

Good time-managers are decisive; poor time-managers are impulsive

Good time-managers decide what they intend to do and then do it. Their actions therefore arise out of their decisions. This is the last thing that a poor time-manager's actions arise out of. A characteristic of poor time-managers is that they have extreme difficulty acting on their decisions. There is always something distracting them. Basically they are reacting to circumstances or just acting on impulse. This is why the mental strength exercise I set you at the end of the Introduction is so important. Being able to do something because you have decided to do it is the foundation of good time-management.

Good time-managers work from the big picture; poor time-managers get bogged down in trivia

Because good time-managers are clear about what their intentions are, they are able to move purposefully towards fulfilling them. Poor time-managers have seldom worked out their intentions clearly and therefore find it very difficult to act purposefully. Without having a big picture to keep their eyes on, they are prey to every kind of trivia. Many of these enter their lives through impulse ('Wouldn't it be a good idea to learn French/surf the net/ go shopping/rearrange the pencils on my desk/take up yoga') or as avoidance activities ('I've been too busy to get around to planning any new initiatives'). There is nothing wrong with any of these activities in themselves of course, but if they are not part of a wider picture they are just unconnected attention-consuming activities without real purpose or synergy with each other.

Good time-managers have good systems; poor time-managers have poor systems or none at all

I mentioned a few paragraphs ago that the most effective people I have ever known shared the characteristic of having a clear desk. There is nothing particularly virtuous about having a clear desk in itself, but the important point is that they both had a good system for dealing with paper. They knew what to do with every bit of paper that came their way. The poor time-manager is constantly receiving paper which he or she has no idea what to do with. So it gets left in a pile or is put unactioned in a drawer 'for later' or even gets thrown away to get it out of sight and out of mind. This doesn't just apply to paper. There is no system for dealing with any type of work. This results in life being led as a series of crises.

Good time-managers keep work and play in balance; poor time-managers have work and play unbalanced – so they both suffer

Effective time-managers take care of their private lives and their recreational time. This is all part of working to the big picture. They know that neither work nor money is an end in itself. They are part of the bigger picture of having a productive and satisfying life. Poor time-managers live compartmentalised lives in which there is little or no synergy. Their lives are therefore condemned to be a constant struggle between the various parts.

Good time-managers are relatively unstressed; poor time-managers make stress a way of life

Because good time-managers act decisively, they are not prey to one of the most stressful factors in most of our lives – procrastination. Avoiding a subject does not get rid of the stress associated with it. It increases it. The result is that bad time-managers are always living with a considerable amount of generalised anxiety. They can often feel this anxiety physically as tension in the body or visualise it as a black cloud hanging over the head. Frequently they only get enough motivation to take action when the stress of not doing something becomes greater than the stress of doing it. Good time-managers, on the contrary, act when resistance is at its lowest, i.e. when action is first seen as necessary.

Good time-managers' attention is focused; poor time-managers' attention is diffused

Once good time-managers have decided to do something, they will give it sufficient attention to bring it to completion and will not let themselves be distracted from doing so. Not so the poor time-managers! A thousand and one things will impinge on their attention, every one a source of anxiety that sets off a chain of impulse reactions.

Good time-managers' response to fear is action; poor time-managers' response to fear is avoidance

Good time-managers know that a certain amount of fear is the natural first reaction to a challenge or new initiative. So they have learned to accept this fear and work through it. In fact they know that if they do not experience some fear they are taking life too easy and are likely to be getting complacent. But with them fear is only a short-lived initial reaction because it is quickly dispersed by taking action. Poor time-managers will do anything to avoid feeling fear. This naturally means that they will tend to avoid challenges or new initiatives which take them out of their comfort zones. They have evolved many different ways of doing so of which the two most popular are procrastination and busyness. Unfortunately all they succeed in doing is to swap an easily dispersible fear for a generalised anxiety which is very difficult to get rid of.

None of the books I read really helped

Fuelled by my own desperation to get organised, I became a devourer of self-help books, particularly those dealing with time-management. I discovered two things about these books. First, they all seemed to cover much the same ground, and second, none of them worked for me. Not consistently, anyway.

Certainly I picked up some useful tips, and I shall be dealing with many of these as we go through this book, but I was still left unable to handle my life effectively and with the anguish and stress of feeling out of control. I wanted so much more and was determined not to accept that I could not win this battle. So I kept on reading and experimenting.

All around me were people who continued to have a problem

with their time, so it seemed obvious to me that the usual time-management recommendations were not working. These people didn't seem to have too much problem with other learned activities. They could read, they could write, they could ride bicycles, drive cars, type on a computer keyboard and use a calculator. Some could play musical instruments. They didn't buy endless books on these subjects and complain that they still couldn't get the hang of them. By and large the techniques for learning these subjects are well established and by adulthood the generality of people don't have too much of a problem with them. But managing our time effectively is a different matter. This is a recurring problem which the generality of people seem to be failing at to a greater or lesser extent, and the successful ones are the exception.

If the techniques commonly taught in time-management books are not producing people who are capable of managing their time successfully, then evidently it is time to take another look at what they are teaching and why it is not effective. This is what I propose to do in this book. Then I aim to give alternative techniques which can lift us out of the problem and give anyone a system they can use. And once having provided this first-aid solution, I will then go on to explore how to go beyond that. Having experienced what it is like to act in spite of resistance, you will then be in a position to use resistance itself as a signpost marking the way to go.

I invented my own techniques and started teaching them to other people

Having started out on my mission to solve my problems with time, I began gradually to find some things that worked. Eventually I made this mission the number one goal in my life because I realised that without solving this time problem, I would never succeed in making anything of my life. I didn't want to come to the end of my life feeling that its predominant motto was 'if only'.

Gradually I began to make progress. I made some false starts, finding techniques which helped but did not lead anywhere. Then I began to look at exactly why most of the recommended techniques didn't work and to see what I could do to improve them. And bit by bit I discovered that I was gaining control, that I could do a large amount of work without getting bogged down, and that at last I could trust myself to finish a project once I had started it. Both my satisfaction in my work and my income rose, and at the same time I was able to spend more time on the subjects which interested me personally.

I had discovered a system which worked for me, and I felt that if it worked for a disorganised person like me it should at the very least give some help to other people in the same situation. So I started to run seminars and to give individual instruction. I found that other people did indeed benefit immensely. And from the feedback that I got I was able to make further refinements.

Then an entirely unexpected thing happened. I began to find that I no longer needed the techniques. Having got the feel for what it was like to have control over my time, I was able to achieve the same feeling without the techniques. I was like someone learning to swim who gets to the stage when they can throw away the water-wings, or like a child learning to ride a bicycle who can take off the training wheels. But if I had not had the techniques in the first place, I would never have reached the stage where I was able to do without them.

Summary

- We cannot manage time – but we can learn to manage how we direct our attention.
- Anything that we give our attention to will start to change.
- Everything changes all the time whether we like it or not. Our choice is whether we are involved in the change or not.
- Good time-managers do something because they have made a

decision to do it; bad time-managers do something because they experience an impulse to do it.

- The ultimate aim is to be able to do what needs to be done when it needs to be done.

Are you doing the mental strength training?

If you have not already started the mental strength exercise that I gave you at the end of the Introduction, make sure that you start it today. This exercise is an essential foundation for enabling you to change from impulse-driven action to decision-driven action – the basis of good time- and life-management.

2

The Need to Manage Our Lives Better

The enormous market for books on personal improvement and on organising one's business or work practices shows how great a need is felt to find an answer to the problems that face us in managing our lives. In this chapter I will be looking at how this need manifests itself and what the results of poor time-management are. We'll also take the opportunity to look at how much of a problem you have in this area.

Time-management is the number one area in which clients ask life-coaches for help

Just as performers in the world of sport have coaches, so the idea of having a coach for the whole of your life is gaining popularity.

A life-coach is someone who can act as source of support, wisdom and guidance in the very individual activity of progressing your own dreams and desires. Life-coaches come in many different forms and specialities, but the one characteristic they all share is that, whether they are primarily coaching you in your business life or your private life, they will encourage you to see your life as one whole.

According to a survey of clients by the International Coaching Federation, time-management is the issue with which clients are most likely to ask their coaches for help. It is even more in demand than career or business development or relationships, areas one would think of as natural fields for coaching. It is perhaps the most prevalent problem that individuals living in Western high-technology societies have. We are simply unable to keep up with the busy lives that modern society thrusts upon us. No matter whether we are men or women, work for a salary or work for ourselves, work in an office, work at home, or work in the field, modern communication and transport have speeded life up to such a degree that we can't keep up. Yes, the potential of our lives has been vastly expanded: we live far wider and less restricted lives than our ancestors; but what does that serve when we feel that we are being spread thinner and thinner over more and more, that the new width has been achieved at the expense of depth? Our lives may be wider but we feel, usually with justification, that they are shallower.

Not that procrastination is a new problem by any means. The proverbial expression 'Procrastination is the thief of time' is actually a quote from a poem by the eighteenth-century poet, Edward Young. And going far further back in time, the biblical Book of Proverbs gives the following graphic warning against idleness.

> A little sleep, a little slumber,
>   a little folding of the hands to rest,
> and poverty will come upon you like a robber,
>   and want, like an armed warrior.
>   (Proverbs 6:10–11)

All through history those who have acted quickly and decisively have been able to seize the advantage over those who merely thought about acting. Julius Caesar was famous for acting so quickly that his opponents were caught completely off guard. Victory after victory was gained because he appeared with his armies long before anyone imagined that it was possible. And when he was finally brought down, it was because his opponents had at last learned the lesson that they needed to act before he did. Unfortunately for them they did not continue to apply the lesson after his death.

As I have already said, we cannot manage time. Time produces exactly twenty-four hours each day whether we like it or not. But it is up to us whether we fill that time with trivia or with worthwhile activities. It is not time we need to manage but ourselves – and particularly we need to learn to manage how and where we focus our attention. Although I will continue to use it in this book when appropriate, the phrase 'time-management' is really a completely inadequate description – what we are in fact dealing with is how we manage our lives. If we were to rename it 'life-management' it might throw a new and clearer perspective on the issue. We are dealing with the surface manifestation of the very roots of our existence and what is important to us.

Inability to manage our attention can ruin our lives or be literally lethal

So what does looking at 'time-management' from the rather different point of view of 'life-management' show us? First of all, that not being able to live our lives the way we want causes us considerable stress and frustration. We can accept that circumstances do not always work out the way we want them to. It is more difficult to accept that failure and poor performance are the result of our own deficiencies, especially when we know that what we were trying to achieve was actually well within our capabilities.

We end up feeling that we are prisoners of our own inability to break out of shackles that we have put in place ourselves. Worse – we realise that we are actively working to maintain and secure those shackles.

Our careers and business suffer from our poor life-management. The successful know how to cut through the many things clamouring for their attention and concentrate on what is really important. We are unable to focus our attention where and when it is needed, and build comfort zones beyond which we are unwilling to progress. The result is that we end up stuck in a rut. It may be a big and beautiful rut but we are stuck in it nonetheless – and inwardly we know it. In the public arena we see examples of this being played out all the time – some stars of popular entertainment are able to reinvent themselves and adapt so that they still keep their appeal. Others are stuck in their original acts and sooner or later fade from the public consciousness.

Poor life-management may also gain us a reputation for unreliability. If our colleagues can't trust us to finish a piece of work it will most certainly not do us any good. It can be annoying or worse to our families if we cannot be relied upon to do what we say we will. I wonder how many divorces are the result not of spectacular acts of cruelty or betrayal but simply the cumulative effect of a constant failure to give each other attention? How many children are estranged because they don't feel their parents care for them? And what does that mean but that the parents have never paid sufficient attention to them as individuals?

So failure to manage our attention can blight our careers, destroy our marriages and alienate our children. What could be worse than that? Well, quite a lot actually. Major accidents and disasters affecting hundreds or thousands of people can be caused or aggravated by simple failure to pay attention.

I have been struck, reading the reports of major accidents, how they are often not the result of one calamitous failure but rather the culmination of a whole series of minor negligences on the part of many people. In the recent earthquakes in Turkey, to take one example, the number of casualties is reported as being greatly increased by the lack of enforcement of building regulations and by the lack of rehearsal of disaster procedures in a zone known to be prone to earthquakes. We can find similar examples of the cumulative effect of negative factors closer to home. A disaster usually has a precipitating cause but it can only precipitate the disaster if many other factors have been neglected. And often if even one of these had not been neglected the results of the accident would have been greatly reduced or eliminated altogether.

And what has led to these little neglects that have added together to cause or aggravate such terrible disasters? Simply procrastination. Most often negligence is not a deliberate decision to neglect to do something, but is just a putting off of paying attention to something that one knows should be done – something that is resisted because it may lead to effort or trouble or both.

Most people show some of the symptoms of poor time-management

I am sure that, if you have read this far, much of what I have said has made sense to you – it has fitted your experience. But here's a quiz to see how many of the symptoms of poor time-management you have. Tick the ones that you feel apply to you enough to be a problem.

- ❑ You are always behind with your work.
- ❑ You have a mass of projects you will get round to 'sometime'.
- ❑ You have so much to do you don't know where to start.
- ❑ The more time you have available the less you get done.
- ❑ If you set aside time for an important project, you fiddle away the time instead of progressing the project.

❑ You start new projects with great enthusiasm but don't carry them through to completion.

❑ You need pressure to build up before you can get motivated to get moving.

❑ You are in a state of constant rush.

❑ When you stop to take a breather, it is ages before you get going again.

❑ There are many things you know in your heart of hearts that you are avoiding giving your attention to.

❑ There are things you have neglected to do that keep you awake at night.

❑ You tend to get carried away by one task to the exclusion of everything else.

❑ You seem to live your life from one crisis to another.

❑ You don't allow proper time for yourself and your family.

❑ You feel you are stretched thinner and thinner over more and more things.

❑ When you finally get round to starting a task which you have been putting off, your attention is distracted by the thought of all the other tasks you haven't yet started on.

❑ You faff around so much during the day that you frequently find yourself working late or bringing work home.

Do any of these sound familiar? Just about everyone feels most of these at some time or other, but if more than a few of these are a regular problem for you then you would probably say that you have a time-management problem. But that's not the real problem – in your heart of hearts you know that however much time you had available you would still not get around to doing everything. You would just find more and more trivia to distract you. What you are really suffering from is not being unable to manage your time, but being unable to manage your attention – not being able to focus it consistently to achieve the results you want. If you are subconsciously avoiding something, your brain is very inventive at finding all sorts of things to keep you from having to tackle it.

Bad time-management affects all areas of our lives

As I have said, the problem has nothing to do with shortage of time. The amount of time we have available is a constant – always exactly the same each day. But the appearance of shortage of time will creep into any area of our lives where there is resistance. It is worth noting here that people with a severe time-management problem in all the rest of their life often have one cherished area in which they have no time problem at all – this may be something like a hobby or a sport or partying – anything which they genuinely enjoy and which therefore provides little or no resistance. If they could live the whole of their lives the way that they live in this one area, their whole way of relating to the world would be transformed.

Our lives tend to flow along the paths of least resistance. An example of how this manifests itself is workaholism. This often occurs because the work environment with its clear-cut framework and supporting structures offers less resistance than the rest of the workaholic's life. If someone is trying to avoid facing up to personal problems, burying themselves in work offers a refuge. In spite of their long hours, workaholics are seldom as effective as they could be in their work. Real effectiveness depends on the ability to cut through to what really matters – and this is just exactly what workaholism is not. Workaholism is often confused with working long hours, but I distinguish between them because there are times when working long hours is definitely necessary. The really effective manager may at times work even longer hours than the workaholic. The difference is that he or she does the work because it is necessary, and only when it is necessary. The workaholic will find work to do whether it is necessary or not. For the effective worker hard work and long hours are a means to a desired end – for the workaholic long hours are an escape from other problems.

Another good example of following the path of least resistance is putting off a task that has a deadline. This of course is a favourite of students with essays or projects to complete. But it applies just as much to people in any other sphere of activity. The more the task is put off the greater the resistance becomes, but also the greater becomes the threat of the impending deadline. Only when resistance to the consequences of missing the deadline becomes greater than resistance to doing the task does any action take place. Note what happens here: the task gets done when the stress associated with it is at its highest. But we always have the choice of doing the task instead at the time when the stress is at its lowest – when it first presents itself to us.

We may have a whole series of tasks over which we are procrastinating, and the effect of this is that we will be in a permanent state of high stress. One extreme way of dealing with this stress is to persuade ourselves that we do not care about the consequences and so fail to do the work at all. Unfortunately reality cannot be thwarted – if we take this attitude the consequences will catch up with us. Our negligence will result in a disaster or crisis, resulting in even more stress. Or more unspectacularly we are condemned for ever to be low achievers.

It is important when we talk about achievement to distinguish between living up to our own expectations and living up to other people's expectations of us. At the end of the day, it is our own expectations that matter. If we don't live up to our own expectations then we will be condemned to a perpetual state of saying 'if only' when we look back on our lives.

Resistance springs up in all areas of our lives. It is just as likely to happen in our personal lives as at work. In fact it is even more likely since our personal lives involve deep emotional relationships with other people far more than our work does. These relationships also have a far greater quality of permanence than our workplace ones. A bad relationship with our boss can be solved by changing jobs. A bad relationship with a member of our immediate family is there for ever unless resolved. 'For ever' can be taken quite literally. Even after their death unresolved conflicts with our parents can poison our lives in many ways. Modern psychology has learnt the truth of the biblical injunction 'Honour your father and your mother, so that your days may be long in the land that the LORD your God is giving you' (Exodus 20:12). Even in cases of gross abuse, forgiving their parents may be one of the most important steps in healing for children. The parents may be long dead and the children in late middle age before this happens.

So the potential for resistance in our personal lives can be very great. We may, as we have seen, be driven to use our work to avoid facing up to problems at home. We neglect these problems until a crisis is provoked and then our work suffers as well.

But perhaps the most distressing result of bad time-management is the waste of our lives. What should be the best and most productive years of our lives pass in a flash and we realise that we have achieved only a small part of what we wanted or what we thought we were capable of. And unless we are able to find a way of making a new start it looks as if we are condemned never to improve – we will not realise our potential during the rest of our lives either.

When we do gain control, our whole lives benefit

I mentioned just now that our lives tend to flow along the path of least resistance. What this in fact means in practice is that the way we live our lives is almost completely the result of outward stimuli. The disapproval of our friends, the constraints of society, the expectations of our parents, the fear of losing financial security, are all more powerful motivators than our own intentions and desires. The predictable channels along which we tend to live our lives do not even have the merit of being our own channels – they have been largely marked out for us by other people.

Learning to manage our time is far wider than just learning to get through a list of tasks as quickly as possible. It is learning to master our own selves – so that we cease merely reacting to life and instead take charge. One of my favourite films is *Groundhog Day*, a fantasy in which the hero played by Bill Murray lives through the same day over and over again until he finally succeeds in winning the heroine's heart and breaking the spell. The lesson I learned from the film is how enormous is the difference in the way a day can turn out according to the actions that we take. The truth is that most of us *are* living the same day over and over again. We take the same limited range of actions each day, and one day turns out in very much the same way as all the others.

For most of us what stops our being very much better people is the same thing that stops our being very much worse people – fear. Fear of the consequences, fear of what people would think, fear of disease or punishment or even death. If we could overcome fear we would find we have an infinity of choices before us. The lesson Bill Murray's character learned was that by breaking out of his habitual ways of reacting, he could make life respond to him.

But we must learn to walk before we can run. And first of all we must learn two things: how to overcome resistance and how to focus our attention. These are the keys to our freedom and they both need practice and training. In the next part of this book we will be examining specific techniques to provide this.

Once we have mastered these we shall be in a better position to reduce or eliminate tension and rushing. We shall no longer be living off adrenaline. We will be able to put our lives back into balance. And most important of all we shall be able to do what we set out to do on a consistent basis.

Summary

- Busyness is often an escape from having to deal with more important and challenging matters.
- Focusing on what is important is the key to success in life.

- Instead of just reacting to life's circumstances, we always have a choice of responses that we can make.
- Learning to overcome resistance sets us free to realise our potential.

Part Two

Techniques

Se io ho ben la tua parola intesa,
   rispose del magnanimo quell'ombra,
   l'anima tua è da viltade offesa,

la qual molte fiate l'uomo ingombra,
   sì che d'onrata impresa lo rivolve,
   come falso veder bestia quand'ombra.

'If I've rightly understood what you're saying,'
   replied that generous soul,
   'you are smitten with cowardice,

'which often obstructs a man
   turning him back from a worthwhile enterprise,
   just like a wild animal frightened by a shadow.'

(Dante, *Inferno* II, 43–48)

Part Two

Techniques

3

The Number One
Time-Management Tool:
Saying No

In this chapter we will explore the most fundamental time-management tool – the word 'no'. As we shall see, we need to learn to say no both to other people and perhaps even more importantly to ourselves. This basic skill is essential – without it we might as well forget about managing our time since any improvement we succeed in making to our ability to process work will only result in our taking yet more work on.

The danger is that better techniques will lead to a bigger and better overwhelm

Every time you let something into your life it becomes a claim on your attention. Your attention is the most valuable commodity you have. We have already seen that time is not a problem – time just is. It is how we allocate our attention that is both the problem and the way out of the problem. It is the way out of the problem because if you give enough of your attention to the problem of how you allocate your attention you will solve the problem. At this very moment you are giving your attention to reading this book. If it is to help you, you will next need to give your attention to putting its contents into practice. This learning to give attention as and when it is required is in itself a large part of the answer.

Imagine that you are living a perfectly organised life in which you are able to give everything you have to do exactly the attention it needs. You decide that you want to allow a new project into your life. To do this successfully you need to reallocate your attention in order to give that new subject its proper place. A previous commitment may have finished, giving the necessary space. But if not, you will need to decide what to stop doing to make room for the new work.

If you do not do this properly, you will not have made space for the project to be given the attention it needs, and your attention will start to be dispersed. The result will be that instead of the focus you previously had, you will not be able to give quite enough attention to anything and your mind will start to get more and more distracted by unfinished business. For many of us this is a fair description of where we already are, and we are usually still in the process of making it more so.

The first step in learning to manage our time has to be to stop adding to the number of things we are already doing. As the next step, we need to work on putting space back into our lives so that we are once again able to give everything the amount of focused attention that it needs. The danger is that we do not face up to the need to go through this essential process. Instead we would prefer to miss out these two steps and go directly to learning techniques for processing work more efficiently.

But the problem with improving our efficiency as a first step is that we shall most likely use the time gained to take on yet more work. So we will end up with the same feeling of overwhelm we had before, only it will be a bigger and better overwhelm. Our new skills in processing trivia more efficiently will have left us no nearer to tackling the things that are really challenging us.

As we have seen, we have an unconscious need for an ever-increasing supply of low-resistance items which serve the purpose of giving us an excuse to avoid having to deal with the more challenging and higher-resistance matters that would really make a breakthrough in our lives and work. As a result most of us have taken on far too much, both in our business and personal lives. Once we start to recognise this overwhelm as what it is – an escape mechanism – we can begin to get free from it.

Almost without exception, my life-coaching clients complain of having too much to do. What they usually want me to do is give them a few new techniques and advise them what priority to give various bits of their work. I will have none of that – the solution needs to be far more radical. My first task is to encourage them to take a machete to the jungle of their commitments and clear out complete areas of their lives. There is tremendous reluctance to do this – I have heard some quite incredible rational-isations for keeping commitments that were patently doing nothing either for them or for the people the commitments were made to. As we have seen, they *need* these activities. Without them they would be forced to face up to the fact that they are unable to confront the major issues in their lives. What has happened is that they have got themselves into a vicious circle in which their efforts to escape from their problems have become worse than the original problems themselves.

I encourage my clients to see their attention as a valuable commodity – the most valuable commodity that they have. I encourage them to set a monetary value on it, to ask themselves: 'How much is an hour of my attention worth to me?' It may be a crude measure but it does serve the purpose of getting them to look at their lives from a different perspective.

Note that I don't say put a value on their *time* – our time is valuable or not valuable according to how much attention we are giving to what we are doing. It is our attention that is valuable. If you are a salaried worker, your employers do not pay you for your time – they are paying you for your attention. If you work for yourself what will forward your business is not how much time you spend on it, but how much attention you give it.

If you are a full-time employee then you can gain a rough measure of the value of your attention by rounding your annual salary to the nearest thousand, knocking off the last three zeros and dividing the remaining figure by two. That will give you a very approximate measure of how much your employers are prepared to pay you for an hour of your attention. So if you are earning £30,000 a year, divide the 30 by two and that gives you a figure of roughly £15 an hour. If *they* consider your attention to be worth that amount then *you* should be putting at least that value on it.

If you are self-employed you can do a similar exercise by thinking how much you want to be earning through your business. If you want to earn £100,000 a year, then your attention is worth £50 an hour to you. It is valuable – do not waste it. If you go to a meeting for an hour and a half and it takes you fifteen minutes to travel to the meeting, then that meeting has taken £100 worth of your attention. Put a value on your attention – its value to you. And cost out the activities you are deploying your attention on.

Exercise

Set a monetary value for an hour of your attention as suggested above. If neither of the above ways of reaching a value apply to you, then just ask yourself what you would be prepared to pay for an hour of uninterrupted time.

Once you have set a value, then work out the cost of the attention you give some of your day-by-day activities. As you go about your daily business, ask yourself whether you would still do this or that activity if you had to pay for it in cash before you did it.

If you complain about paying the licence fee for your television, it is useful to remember that watching the news may be costing you £25 worth of your attention every day. I am not of course saying that there is anything wrong with watching the television news. All I want you to do is ask yourself whether you are getting value out of it.

An old saying is that you can do *anything* if you put your mind to it, but you can't do *everything*. Life presents us with an infinity of choices. But the very fact that we call them 'choices' shows that we can't have all of them. An essential part of coming to maturity is making the choices and commitments that are going to shape our lives. That does not mean that these choices are engraved in stone and that we can never change them. What it does mean is that we all have to go through a process of choosing what to give our attention to and what *not* to give our attention to.

To do this effectively means making conscious decisions. Unfortunately we often fail to say 'no' properly to the infinity of possible choices that the world presents us with. This is often because we have failed to say a definite 'yes' to those things we *have* decided on. The classic example is the philanderer who is unable to commit fully to one woman but goes chasing after every available woman who appears on the scene. All of us, men and women, are liable to have many will-o'-the wisps we go chasing after because we have never decided what we really are committed to. It is a point worth noting that the number of things we are not committed to is by the very nature of things always going to vastly outnumber the things we are committed to. When we order a meal in a restaurant, there are a huge number of possible combinations of meals that we could eat but we still have to make a choice of the one meal that we are actually going to eat.

It is our refusal to accept this very simple fact that leads to our spreading our attention over so many areas that we do not have sufficient left to do any of them properly.

Before I teach you any techniques, it is absolutely imperative that you look at your life and decide what you intend to give your attention to. Remember you can always change your priorities –

what you cannot do is give more attention than you have attention to give.

Here is an exercise to start you on the process of making these decisions. You may need to come back to it several times – I would advise you to make it a regular commitment to keep it under revision. This is an essential preliminary exercise because without it the rest of this book will only make you a more efficient processor of trivia rather than a really effective human being.

Exercise

1 Write out a list of all the areas of commitment and activity you have in your life. Include your work and your personal life. Break them down as far as possible so that you have categorised all your areas of endeavour. Don't forget to include all commitments you have – to parents, children, friends, charities, etc. Also include rest and recreational activities. In other words make a detailed list of everything that you feel has a claim on your attention at the moment, regardless of whether you are currently succeeding in giving it any attention or not.

2 Now against each item on the list, write down approximately what percentage of your time you are giving it at the moment. You do not have to be completely accurate, but make an effort to get as good a picture as possible. Spend some time adjusting the percentages to get them in the right balance. Obviously they must add up to 100. Your attention is finite – it is not possible to give more than 100 per cent of your attention.

3 So far the exercise has been reasonably easy. Now comes the difficult bit. You have to ensure that every item is being given *sufficient* attention to do it properly. And of course the total still has to come to 100 per cent. Most of us have so many things on our plates that to do them properly would require far more of our attention than we have. The result is that some of them (and very likely most of them) do not get done properly. The only way to get this equation to come out is to strike items off the list. You can do this either by giving them to someone

else to do (possibly paying them) or by deciding not to do them at all. IMPORTANT: at this stage this is just an exercise. Don't start making major changes in your life yet because we need to do some more work on it.

4 The point of this exercise is to get you to face up to the fact that you only have a limited amount of attention and that it is pointless to take on activities that you don't have time to do properly. What 'doing something properly' means is that you give it enough attention to achieve your aims for it. What your aims are is up to you. There is obviously a great deal of difference between deciding to win an Olympic gold medal and going for a jog every other day to keep you reasonably fit. The activity – running – is the same in each case; the aims are very different. But both the gold medal and the fitness jogging need to be allocated the attention that is appropriate for them.

5 When you have finished this exercise you should have a list in which every item has sufficient attention to ensure that it is done properly *and* the total of your attention is no more than 100 per cent. Keep your workings so you can refer to them again later.

This is not an easy exercise, but if you do it properly it will force you to face up to the finite nature of your attention and how important it is to direct it intelligently. You may have to make some hard choices to make your list come out. Some things you may have reluctantly to give up in the knowledge that for the time being at least you cannot give them the attention they deserve. Other things you may discover you can give up without any reluctance at all. You may have to acknowledge the fact that some things are indeed essential but you do not have adequate resources to do them yourself – in which case you may need to delegate them or hire someone to do them for you.

As I mentioned earlier, you are unlikely to arrive at the perfect answer first time round. But it will get your mind working on the sort of changes you need to make. Above all, remember that it is better to do a few things well than a lot of things badly.

Learning to say no to low-value activities is essential

Ultimately only you can decide what value your various activities are to you. The value you give to something depends on what your values in life are. What is valuable to me may have little value to you and vice versa.

The terrible truth, though, is that most of us spend a very large part of our day on activities that have very little value for us. Often these are obligations we have taken on at the request of other people because we did not see how we could say no or because we felt we ought to do them. In these cases we have allowed someone else's values to supplant our values. But very often what is really happening is that we have loaded ourselves with low-value but easy-to-do activities to shield ourselves from having to do high-value but difficult activities. Either way the first step is to see that the reason we are letting these activities into our lives is as an escape, as a method of avoidance. If we are quite clear about what our values are, then we are much less likely to accept things into our lives that do not contribute to those values.

So before taking on any new activity or commitment ask yourself 'What am I doing at the moment that has less value to me than this?' Remember that at the moment you are already filling every day with twenty-four hours' worth of activities. If you are going to introduce another activity, then something you are already doing has to go. We tend to take on new activities without thinking about this self-evident fact. We like to think that time will just somehow expand to take in the newcomer.

I would like to make something clear here. I have talked a lot about looking at what value something has to us. I do not want you to think by that I mean that you should take an entirely self-centred view of life. In fact I mean quite the opposite. Our values may include our families, service to the community, spirituality and other issues that are much wider than our own narrow advantage. In fact we would not be leading very fulfilling lives if our values were purely self-centred and did not include other people. What I am saying is that our attention should be given to what is important to us – only we can decide what that is.

Exercise: 'Collecting Noes'

When asked to do something, most of us have a tendency to say 'yes' with reluctance and then regret it. In this way we can accumulate innumerable commitments without really wanting any of them.

The aim of this exercise is to reverse this so that our initial reaction is to say 'no' to every request rather than 'yes'. Make a game of it. See how many times you can say 'no' during the day. In order to say 'no' effectively you need to use the right techniques:

1 Always use a neutral tone of voice when saying 'no' – never sound annoyed, shamefaced or harassed.
2 Be prepared to repeat your 'no' at least once.
3 Never give an excuse – if you do you will find yourself having to defend it.
4 Say something on the lines of 'I appreciate you asking me, but I can't fit that into my priorities at the moment'. Don't elaborate. If challenged, repeat it in the same neutral tone of voice. It's all right to give a reason such as 'I am concentrating right now on getting our new project completed'. The more general the reason is, the less easy it is for someone to shoot it down.
5 If it's your boss doing the asking, try 'I can't fit that into the work priorities I have at the moment. Is there something you'd like me to put on hold for the moment so I can fit this in?' Again don't forget the neutral tone of voice!
6 If after saying 'no' you change your mind and decide you'd really like to do it after all, that's great! The point is that you are doing it because you want to and not because you feel you ought to.

So start collecting your 'noes'. You will be surprised what a good feeling it gives you!

Janet

Janet is a single mother with a nine-year-old daughter. She is in partnership with a friend of hers in their own business. She has a very lively and inventive mind and is also an extremely social person. She loves organising things and as a result was always starting up new meetings, societies and appeals for a whole variety of different causes. At work she was continually coming up with new initiatives and projects.

When she came to me for advice, she was complaining that she was finding that things she used to enjoy doing were no longer as much fun as they used to be. In fact she was feeling generally harassed and her work was suffering too.

My first task was to get her to concentrate on making an inventory of what was really important to her.

'My daughter obviously is most important to me. We're around a lot together but too often we're just sharing the same space because I'm busy working at something. I would really like to be able to spend more time doing things specifically with her and giving her my sole attention.

'My work's very important to me too. But it's the same story again – I have lots of ideas but don't have the time to put them into effect. And we've got a lot of projects that need more work on them, but we just get submerged.

'And I really want to be able to contribute, to feel that I'm putting something back. I would never want to be living just a selfish life.

'And then I need some sort of social life, and in the back of my mind is always the thought that I might get married again – but at the moment I don't stand still long enough for anyone to meet me!'

She was very reluctant to allow that anything she was doing could be cut back. Especially she felt that cutting her community work would turn her into a selfish person and she would 'never allow that'.

Once she started looking at the way she was spending her time, she was able to see that everything she was doing was in competition for a share of her life. The only way one thing could get done properly was by another thing being neglected. The message really got home to her when we concentrated on what was most important to her – her daughter. 'Is it selfish to make sure that you give your daughter the attention she needs?' I asked. She agreed that it was far from selfish – it was the most important thing she could do at this stage of her daughter's life.

By working her way through the things that were important to her and making sure that everything was given adequate time, she was finally able to make some crucial decisions. Having decided how much quality time she was going to give her daughter, she then got together with her business partner and together they agreed to restrict the number of projects they had to a number they could handle successfully. In particular they agreed that they must always get one initiative fully established before starting on another. At the same time they decided to take on a part-time employee to handle some of the routine work. Janet also made a strict rule to stop working late. She said: 'Working late has become a bad habit. It's not really necessary but somehow I've just slipped into it.'

By this time she had realised that there was no way that she could justify keeping the plethora of commitments she had built up within her local church and community. I had encouraged her to look at the real cost to her in time of even the smallest commitment, and the exercise had horrified her. With great reluctance, she made a decision to concentrate on just one project and to resign from all the others. 'I dreaded people's reactions, but in fact they were remarkably understanding when I explained I needed to find more time with my daughter. And once I got rid of the feeling of being harassed all the time, I realised how much I had been resenting the demands on me.' She found that she was able to work far more effectively on the one project that she had kept.

Action summary

- Reduce your commitments until you are able give everything the attention it needs.
- Remember: every time you take on a new commitment, you have to *stop* doing something you are doing at the moment.
- Make 'No' your instinctive first response to any request.
- Learn how to say no in a neutral tone of voice.
- Give a reason rather than an excuse and make it relate to one of your key values (e.g. 'I am concentrating on spending more time with my daughter' rather than 'I haven't got the car on Thursday evenings').

Interlude – A Fairy Story

Once upon a time in a far-off land a merchant's son fell in love with a beautiful princess. Merchants' sons in fairy stories always seem to be called Hans, so we will call him that. Now since the king was short of money, as kings in fairy stories always are, he was quite happy for Hans to court his daughter as Hans's father was very rich.

Unfortunately just after Hans had succeeded in attracting the princess's attention, Hans's father decided it was time to retire and he left his business to Hans. Hans found himself so busy that he didn't have time to deal with all the business affairs and court the princess too.

In despair he remembered that in the village lived an old wizard who was reputed to know everything that was to be known. So Hans went to the wizard's cottage and told the wizard his problem.

'Prioritise, my son,' said the wizard. 'That's the secret. Do what's most important first.'

Hans was overjoyed to receive such good advice. There was no doubt in his mind what was his number one priority

– it was the beautiful princess. So every day he climbed on his horse and rode over to the castle and spent the day wooing the princess. Unfortunately one day his horse went lame because Hans hadn't bothered to get a loose shoe fixed – horseshoes were very low on his list of priorities. So Hans had to walk. And then he himself went lame because he hadn't got round to having his boots mended – boots were very low priority too. So Hans couldn't go and see his princess at all. To make things worse his business was now doing badly because of all his absence and he had to spend much more time than ever trying to put it right.

Hans was in despair again. But then he remembered that there was another wizard who lived deep in the forest that lay beside the village. This wizard was reputed to know even more than the first wizard, if that were possible. So Hans hired a replacement horse at great expense and went to see this wizard.

'Do it now!' said the wizard. 'That's the secret – do it now! If you'd got your horse's shoe fixed as soon as you'd noticed it was loose you wouldn't have had the problem. Same thing with your boots. Do it now!'

Hans's heart leaped within him at receiving such wonderful advice. As soon as he got home, he started doing everything now. He sent his boots off to the cobbler and his horse to the farrier. He wrote up the bills for his customers immediately and took care to file away the receipt from the bank for the takings. He wrote a letter to his parents which he'd been meaning to write for weeks. He even remembered to post it! That night he went to bed with a light heart.

The next morning while he was shaving he noticed that

there was a crack in the mirror. 'Do it now!' he said to himself. So he was about to set off to the mirror shop to buy a new mirror when he noticed that the gutter outside his house was dripping. 'Do it now!' he said. So he got a ladder and climbed up to see what was the problem. While he was up there he noticed a man going past who owed him some money. 'Do it now!' he said, and rushed down the ladder to speak to the man. But as he did so, he remembered he was supposed to be buying a mirror. 'Do it now!' he said and set off for the mirror shop again.

By the end of the day, Hans had half-done lots of minor jobs, but he hadn't spent any time on his business and, worst of all, he hadn't written to the princess.

Hans was in despair again. But he remembered there was an even more powerful wizard who lived high up the foothills behind the village. So Hans hired a guide and two donkeys at even greater expense, and climbed up the hills to the wizard's hut.

'The secret is to list everything you have to do,' said the wizard, 'then number all the items in the order you are going to do them. Then cross them off the list one by one as you do them.'

Again Hans was overjoyed at receiving such wonderful advice. He went down the hill, and started his list. Because he had been neglecting things so much it was a very long list. But he numbered it and started working on it. It was a tremendous feeling crossing things off the list. He enjoyed it so much that he started thinking of more things to put on the list. Gradually the list got longer and longer. For every one item that he did, he added at least another three. At the end of the day when he wrote out the list for the next day it was twice as long as his original list.

After a couple of days, it seemed to Hans that he was spending more time writing out the list than he was spending working on the items. So despair gripped his heart again.

But a friend of his told him of an even more powerful wizard who lived, not in the foothills like the previous wizard, but at the top of the very highest mountain in the range. This time Hans had not only to hire a guide and donkeys but some tents and porters as well. It wasn't till the end of the fourth day of climbing that he reached the wizard's cave. He poured out his heart to the wizard.

'Your problem is easily solved,' said the wizard. 'Make a list as you did before but put in the exact time you are going to do each item. That way you will know exactly what you can fit into each day. Schedule your time, my son – that is the solution.'

This seemed the most wonderful advice that Hans had received yet. He rushed back down the mountain on his donkey, drew up his list again, worked out how long each item would take and scheduled the next day from getting up in the morning to going to bed at night. The first day went swimmingly. He went to bed that night having achieved more in one day than he ever had in his life before. The second day was even better. The third day he was just finishing the twenty-five minutes he had allocated for lunch, when a carriage turned up at the door with an invitation from the princess to spend the afternoon with her at the castle. Now Hans had scheduled in that he would write to the princess from 3.20 p.m. to 3.55 p.m. so, as the princess's invitation didn't fit into his schedule, he sent the carriage back empty to the castle.

As the carriage disappeared round the corner, Hans

realised what he had done. He remembered the whole point of trying to manage his time was so that he could woo the princess. Here was a priceless opportunity and he had rejected it because it didn't fit into his schedule. Suddenly scheduling didn't work any more for him. He couldn't make himself stick to the times and interruptions seemed to come at him from every direction. He was seized with despair again.

Unfortunately he seemed to have run out of wizards. But then he remembered that he had heard a rumour about an incredibly powerful one who lived on top of a column in the middle of the desert that stretched beyond the mountain range. This time he had to set up a complete expedition, and to do so he had to mortgage his house and sell his business. After weeks and months of terrible hardship he found the wizard on top of his column, and poured out his troubles to him.

'Do the thing you most fear first,' was all the wizard said. Hans realised that this was indeed the key he had been seeking for. Full of joy he made the long journey back to his home. 'What is the thing I fear most?' he asked himself. 'Of course, to ask the princess's hand in marriage.'

The trouble was that he was so terrified at the idea that he couldn't bring himself to do it. And until he did it, he knew he mustn't do anything else. So he sat at home, paralysed with fear, doing nothing. Eventually his house was repossessed as he hadn't made any payments on the mortgage.

'I've got nothing to lose now,' he said. 'I will go to the castle and ask for her hand right this minute.' So he limped painfully along the road (his expeditions hadn't exactly improved his lame foot) and arrived at the castle. He staggered into the princess's presence and asked her to marry him. She looked at the ragged, unshaven, unwashed young man and turned him down flat.

Broken-hearted, Hans started on his way back to the village. On his way, through his tears he saw a man walking slowly along the road towards him. By now he was pretty good at recognising a wizard when he saw one and his heart leaped within him as he realised this looked like a quite exceptionally powerful one.

The wizard was very sympathetic. 'Your trouble, my son, is that you have been trying to resist life instead of surrendering to it. Forget all this stuff the other wizards have been telling you. Just go with the flow. Let life take you where it will. Live for the moment. Follow the path of least resistance.'

Of all the wizardly help Hans had received, this seemed the most wonderful of wonderful advice. Thanking the wizard profusely, he continued along the road to the village. As he passed the village tavern, he definitely felt that the path of least resistance led through its door. And in the tavern Hans learned how to surrender to life, and he forgot all about the princess.

As for the princess, she married a handsome prince who had servants to do all the work.

4

Common Time-Management Methods

Let us now turn our attention to examining the advice which the wizards in my fairy story gave to Hans – which is basically the advice that is found in most time-management books. The difficulties Hans found when he tried to follow this advice are an exaggerated version of the problems most of us have trying to follow it too. The continuing difficulty most people have with managing their lives suggests that the standard time-management methods are not effective in the majority of cases. That is not to say they are entirely without value. What I want to do in this chapter is to see why these methods do not work in spite of sounding good, and how we can nevertheless get much value out of them provided we know what their limitations are.

Most common time-management methods don't work on a consistent basis

During the years in which I read time-management book after time-management book I found the same themes came back time after time. They might be dressed up in different ways, but usually at bottom each book contained much the same advice as most of the others. I gradually became convinced that the reason that most people continue to have time-management problems is that these methods are flawed. Although they sound good, they do not in fact work consistently. That is not to say they don't work for some people or that they have no value in them. But for the great majority of us who have real problems with directing our attention they simply do not deliver the goods.

The Hans fairy story gave a representative selection of the most common of these methods and I want to look at each one of them individually in some detail. I will be showing what each one's drawbacks are because I believe it is important to understand why they don't work. Also while I look at each one, I will draw out what we can learn from it that is valuable and in what circumstances it would be useful. Some of the lessons learned we will be able to put to good use straight away, and some will have to wait until a later section of this book.

Here is a summary of the advice that Hans received from the wizards:

* prioritise;
* do it now;
* make to-do lists;
* schedule your day;
* do the thing you fear most first;
* go with the flow.

Each of these sounds good – indeed Hans was delighted as he received each one of them. If you have used any of these methods in the past you can probably remember being delighted when you first came across the principle. But, like Hans, you have probably found that putting it into practice is not so easy. Most people blame themselves for this, rather than questioning whether the principle is right in the first place. So let us start with the first bit of advice that Hans received – perhaps the most common of all.

Prioritise

Prioritising is the sacred cow of time-management methods. I don't think I have ever read a time-management book that didn't advise some form of prioritising one's work. Even to suggest that prioritising work is the wrong approach brings gasps of disbelief – very often from the very same people who consistently fail at prioritising. Their attitude seems to be that prioritising is what one *should* do – and if one is incapable of doing it properly that is because one is a failure as a human being, not because the method itself is wrong.

I can hear you saying: 'Just a minute, the exercise you gave us in the last chapter was an exercise in prioritising.' To which my reply is: 'No, that's exactly what it wasn't. It was an exercise in choices, not priorities.' If you did the exercise properly, what you ended up with was not a prioritised list but simply a list – a list of things you have chosen to give your attention to. Again, if you did the exercise properly, you should have sufficient time available to give adequate attention to every item on your list. This is quite different from a prioritised list in which you are rationing out your attention so that some items get adequate attention and some do not.

One problem with trying to tackle one's work by prioritising it is that there are usually simply too many things that need to be done. Let us take an example. In your work you are working on Project A, Project B and Project C. If you start prioritising between them the inevitable result will be that one or other of the projects (or very likely all three) won't get done properly. The real way forward would be to cut out one of the projects altogether so there was adequate time available for both the remaining projects. The remaining projects can then be given equal priority.

This is a very simplified example, but it illustrates a basic fact about allocating our attention. The real question is not what priority something is, but whether it should be done at all. That is so important I will say it again: **The real question is not what priority something is, but whether it should be done at all.** If we don't have the resources to do all the projects we have in hand, then the only really satisfactory solution is to cut the number of projects until they match the resources we have available.

Once we have decided that something needs to be done, then it needs to be done. If we decide that we are going to commit ourselves to carrying out Project A, then all the work associated with Project A must be done. There can be no question of prioritising some and neglecting some. For example if we start thinking that contacting clients is higher priority than paying attention to having a good filing system, we will end up by having our records in such chaos that we start losing clients.

If we have rigorously asked the question 'Should this be done at all?', then everything we do will be an essential contribution towards our overall goals. No part of what we do can be considered of less priority. Nearly two thousand years ago St Paul made the same point when talking about the members of the infant Christian church:

If all were a single member, where would the body be? As it is there are many members, yet one body. The eye cannot say to the hand, 'I have no need of you,' nor again the head to the feet, 'I have no need of you.' On the contrary, the members of the body that seem to be weaker are indispensable. (1 Corinthians 12:19–22)

If we classify some of our work as 'weaker' (i.e. low priority) and neglect it, we will discover soon enough just how indispensable it really is. Unglamorous administrative tasks, or whatever, are just as important to the overall result as the so-called 'high-priority' items. If the supporting tasks are not done, the high-priority work will eventually collapse.

Exercise

Go back to the exercise on p. 38 and revise it in the light of what I have been saying about priorities. Be bold about throwing out entire projects. Try several alternative scenarios and see which you feel happiest with. Remember this is an exercise in *choice*. Look at it as if you were choosing the items off a restaurant menu. You are in charge!

IMPORTANT: at this stage this is still just an exercise. In a moment we will be doing a little bit more work on it, and then you will be ready to start putting it into effect.

Having spent some time demolishing the whole idea of prioritising, I am now going to say that there are times when prioritising is both useful and necessary. This is when it is a matter of prioritising on grounds of *urgency* rather than *importance*. Usually this applies when a crisis or emergency situation occurs. If you are giving the right amount of attention to all aspects of your work, then crises and emergencies should only occur rarely. They are usually the result of a lack of attention somewhere. But they will occur from time to time whatever we do. Hence we need to be capable of responding to them.

A typical scenario would be this. You have just arrived at work. You have a fairly busy morning ahead of you which includes the final preparations for an important meeting that afternoon at which you are giving a presentation. You have left things a bit to the last minute, but nevertheless know you have enough time to get ready for the presentation and deal with various other pressing matters that are awaiting your attention. As you get down to work, the phone rings. It is one of your most important clients with an emergency request which has to be dealt with there and then. As you put the phone down, you realise that you suddenly have not got the faintest idea how you are going to get everything done before the meeting. You start to panic. You feel paralysed.

You may not have been in these precise circumstances but I am sure you recognise the feeling of panic that hits us when we suddenly find we have run out of enough time to get something finished. In our example the danger is that you will start running around like a headless chicken, and end up arriving upset and poorly prepared to give your presentation.

The first step in dealing with a situation like this is to reduce the feeling of generalised panic by specifying your fear. Specific fears are less immobilising than generalised unspecified fears. You can do this very easily by writing out a list of everything you have to do. Simply writing it down quantifies the fear and reduces the panic.

The next step is to use a simple system of prioritising the items on your list. The one I have found most effective in this sort of situation is to grade them according to the following code:

A – MUST DO
B – SHOULD DO
C – COULD DO

These priorities need to be made within the context of a specific time period. In other words what *must* you do before your meeting, what *should* you do before your meeting and what *could* you do before it if you had time? Once you have graded everything on your list, start working on the most urgent of the A items – the ones you *must* do. This may include asking other people to do some of the items for you.

Now it is important to understand that this is a method for dealing with a crisis. It will not work for our everyday life. The reason for this is very simple: in any one day we will probably never get further than part of the way through the SHOULD DOS. The next day there will be another set of MUST DOS and more SHOULD DOS. This means that the only way that the COULD DOS will ever get done is if they get neglected so much that they become MUST DOS. In other words what we are doing is putting things off until they either die completely or become emergencies. Which is a pretty good description of the way most of us work already! Don't worry – by the end of this book you will have learnt some better ways.

Exercise

This exercise comes in two parts.

Part One

1 Make a list of everything you have to do over the next working week. Include things you do every day and things you keep saying you'll do but haven't got round to doing yet. Don't worry whether you have enough time for it all or not.

2 Now prioritise the list using MUST DO, COULD DO and SHOULD DO in the way I have suggested above. Prioritise it relative to tomorrow (or the next working day) only. So what *must* you do tomorrow? What *should* you do tomorrow? Everything else comes in the COULD DO category.

3 Examine your list of COULD DOs. Accept the fact that you will probably never get round to doing most of them while they remain COULD DOs. Which ones will die away and which ones will become emergencies if left? Specify which are which.

Part Two

1 Take the same list (write it out again if necessary) and this time prioritise it by importance. How you decide what is important is up to you. Put a 1 against the most important item on the list, a 2 against the second most important and so on for the whole list.

2 Now from your knowledge of your own past experience, answer this question as honestly as you can before you look at the list again. What proportion of the items on your list are you actually likely to do during the coming week – 100 per cent (unlikely since you wouldn't need to be reading this book)? 60 per cent? 20 per cent?

3 Whatever proportion you decide on, work out how many items that represents on your list. For example if you have a list of fifty items and you decide you are likely to do 40 per cent of them in a week, that would represent twenty items that you are likely to have succeeded in doing by the end of the week.

4 Tick off the items that you will have done by the end of the week if your forecast comes out right. Then examine the items that you will not have done. Again accept the fact that most of these are never going to get done if they stay at the same level of importance. As you did in Part One, specify which are likely to become emergencies and which are likely to simply die from neglect.

In the two parts of the exercise you have just done, you prioritised your list first by urgency and, second, by importance. And you got a similar result each time: some things are going to become emergencies and the rest will die from lack of attention.

My purpose in these two exercises is to drive home the fact that if you have too many commitments there is no system of prioritisation that will make it possible for you to give proper attention to all of them. If you have too much work, prioritising does not work. And if you don't have too much work, prioritising is not necessary.

So far I have advised you not to make any major changes in your life as a result of doing these exercises, apart from avoiding taking on yet more responsibilities by practising saying 'no'. But now you have reached the stage where you can start making some rearrangements. I suggest you revise the exercise on p. 38 again for the third time – this time with the intention of actually cutting out some of your commitments. Take this process slowly and keep it under review as you read the rest of this book.

Do it now

Another favourite of time-management experts is the phrase 'Do it now'. Often this is combined with such ideas as that one should only handle each piece of paper once. Now I do agree that 'Do it now' is an excellent principle in certain circumstances. For instance in my younger and more irresponsible days I used to have a problem with filling my car with petrol. As the tank got near empty I would pass a filling station and decide I did not need to fill up yet. I would pass another and decide the same thing. Until the inevitable happened – I found myself desperately looking for a filling station with the needle hovering on empty. On a couple of occasions I did indeed succeed in running out of petrol. But now I have a rule that whenever that little yellow warning light comes on I fill up at the next station without fail.

Another example is that when I came back from an evening meeting I used to have a bad habit of just throwing my papers into a pile and forgetting about them – with the inevitable result that action I had agreed at the meeting got mislaid or overlooked. Now, using the 'Do it now' principle, I always make sure that papers are put away and action flagged up for the next day. It takes five minutes or less but makes all the difference in efficiency.

So 'Do it now' is an extremely useful mindset when establishing systems and routines which ensure that work and personal life run smoothly. But both my examples have one common characteristic – there is no doubt what the next step should be. The action to which I am applying 'Do it now' in these two examples is the next step in a previously decided or self-evident chain of actions. In other words the phrase is a way of encouraging me not to deviate from a clearly marked-out path.

The problem comes when we are dealing with actions that are not part of a set routine. If we are told that 'Do it now' is the way forward, we need to ask the question of what 'it' is. At any one time we are faced with a thousand and one things we could be doing. The second we decide to do one thing now, we are at the same moment deciding that we are not going to do the other thousand possible things now. It is a question of selectivity. How do we decide *what* it is that we should be doing now? If, like Hans, what we do is to respond to whatever happens to present itself at any given moment, we will only succeed in burying ourselves in yet more trivia.

'Do it now' may not in any case be the best way to handle many things. It is more sensible to tackle all aspects of our lives systematically than to be constantly leaping here and there in order to 'Do it now'. A more effective way may be deliberately *not* to do something now but to defer it so it can be dealt with at a later stage along with other similar items. We will be exploring this as we go through this book.

'Do it now' is an important concept for good life management provided it is used properly. I will be returning to it again in the final chapters of this book as we get nearer to our final aim of doing the right thing at the right time without having to think about it. But we have a long way to go before we get there.

To-do lists

Just as I have never yet read a book on time-management or personal organisation which does not advocate prioritising, so I have also never read one which does not advocate some form of to-do list. To-do lists and prioritising seem to be the staple fare of most time-management systems. But the awful reality is that most people who set out to keep a to-do list fail to do so on any consistent basis. And those who do succeed often seem to become prisoners of their list – unable to see life in any terms other than ticking off items from the list.

I want to make it clear that I make a fundamental distinction between to-do lists and checklists. A checklist is a list of smaller tasks needed in order to carry out a bigger task. A shopping list is an everyday example of a checklist. Further examples would include:

- making a list of points to raise during a phone call;
- breaking down the action steps for a new project;
- laying down an efficient routine for staff cleaning hotel bedrooms;
- listing action agreed with a customer;
- points to note when carrying out a fire safety check.

Checklists are essential for efficient working. Whenever you start work on a new task it is a good idea to write a quick checklist of the action needed. Apart from anything else, writing a checklist reduces the resistance to the task itself. Smaller tasks are less daunting than bigger tasks.

But a to-do list is a different animal altogether. Whereas a checklist is a list of tasks *relating to a specific larger task or project*, a to-do list is a list of *unrelated* tasks that could be done in a particular space of time, usually a day.

As we have seen, the biggest problem with to-do lists is that, whatever system of prioritising is used, a sizeable proportion of the tasks will not get done within the time period and will need carrying forward to the next one. Since the tasks on a to-do list are unrelated to each other, the human mind is only too good at thinking up new tasks to go on the list. The result of all this is that to-do lists tend to get longer and longer. They take on a bigger and bigger load of items which are carried forward from day to day. This can only go on so long before the list gets torn up in frustration and the list-keeper breathes a sigh of relief at the new sense of freedom from the tyranny of the list.

Exercise

Part One

Take a fairly straightforward project you have been putting off for some time. Decide that you are going to get started on it today. Write a checklist of the action that needs to be done to complete that task. If any of the tasks still seem daunting to you, then break them down further. Go away and do at least one item on the list. Note how much less resistance you feel to doing one small task than to the whole project.

Part Two

When you have done that, look again at the checklist you made in Part One of the exercise. See if there are any actions you could add to the list to ensure the project is done as completely as possible. Try to find at least two or three.

What I want you to notice from this exercise is that adding items to a checklist *increases* the effectiveness and easiness of the checklist. The more you break the project down, the more thoroughly it will be done and the easier each individual item is.

This contrasts with adding items to a to-do list, which *reduces* its effectiveness and easiness because the more items you have on it the more unmanageable the list becomes.

Scheduling

Scheduling is rather like having a to-do list with times attached. You don't just write out a list of actions but also decide *when* you are going to do them. This does have the great advantage that it forces you to look realistically at how much you can really do in a day and to make the necessary choices.

Scheduling is also the way that the very rich, successful or powerful of this world live their lives. If you are the Queen or the Pope or a movie superstar, a large part of your life is run by schedule. So we tend to think that if that is the way people with money or status run their lives then we will become more like them if we do the same.

The problem with this idea is that being able to live by schedule is the *result* of being rich or powerful or both, not the cause. People like this have managers, assistants and other staff to plan for them and ensure that their schedules happen as intended. You don't find the President of the United States searching in a panic-stricken way through a pile of papers trying to find the envelope on which he has jotted down the time his aeroplane leaves for his state visit to France.

For the rest of us there are two major difficulties with trying to schedule our lives. The first is that life is unpredictable. The second is that putting time aside to do something doesn't mean that we will actually do it.

Interruptions and emergencies are going to occur. If we are wise we will have built extra time into our schedule to allow for this. But even so we are inevitably going to find that our schedule will get thrown off and we will have to rewrite it. At times it can seem that we spend more time rewriting our schedules than we spend on the tasks. So the first problem with a schedule is its inflexibility. It is not good at coping with interruptions, crises or emergencies.

The second drawback of a schedule is that it frequently does not need a crisis or interruption to throw it off. We are quite capable of throwing our schedules off all by ourselves. Writing down that we are going to work on a particular subject at a particular time is all very well – but it doesn't necessarily help us to get started on the subject or prevent us from spinning our wheels.

Just as I make a fundamental distinction between a to-do list and a checklist, so I make an equally fundamental distinction between a schedule and a programme. A schedule, like a to-do list, is made up of unrelated actions. A programme is a list of timings relating to a specific larger task, just as a checklist is a list of items relating to a larger task. And like a checklist, the more comprehensive and detailed a programme is the more effective it will be.

Programming is a very effective way of organising our time when we have a specific appointment to keep. People who have chronic problems of lateness can often go a long way to over-coming them by programming the immediate period leading up to the appointment.

Programming is essential whenever you are co-ordinating your activities to fit the activities of one or more other people. The time-programme provides the framework by which more than one person can be at the same place or using the same means of communication in order to achieve a common task.

Exercise

If you have a tendency to turn up late for meetings, then try programming the lead-up to your next meeting. If the meeting starts at 11 a.m. what time do you want to arrive in order not to be rushed? What time do you need to set out in order to achieve that? What time do you need to stop working on other things in order to leave on time? This is usually the crucial point – if you can stop working on other things at the right time you will have greatly improved your likelihood of turning up at the meeting on time. I will be covering this in greater detail in a later chapter.

Do the thing you fear most first

Another piece of advice commonly met with is to draw up your list of tasks for the day and then select the task that you most fear doing and get that out of the way first. The theory is that once you have got your biggest fear out of the way everything else will seem relatively easy.

This advice does contain a great deal of truth. Just as I shall be returning to 'Do it now' to build on it in a more advanced context, so I will with this advice too. In fact I believe this advice, slightly adjusted, is one of the keys to the highest levels of managing our attention.

But the problem is that this advice is usually given to people who are still at relatively low levels of competency in managing their attention. In particular they have not yet learned *how* to overcome resistance in even its most obvious and least insidious forms. To tell someone who has a problem with procrastination 'Do the thing you fear most first' is like telling someone who is taking adult literacy classes that if they read Joyce's *Ulysses* they would find everything else easy. To attempt something which is beyond our capabilities doesn't stretch us so much as discourage us.

The result of this advice is usually that after a few days the person ends up doing nothing at all because they cannot bring themselves to get that first item done. Then they despair of all attempts to organise themselves and go back to their original state of disorganisation.

Another subtler objection is that what we fear most is not necessarily what we are resisting most. We may fear making a difficult phone call to an unsatisfied customer, but what we are resisting is taking a deep look at the reasons why we are upsetting customers in the first place. This difference between what we are fearing and what we are resisting is a crucial one – and I will be exploring it in the final chapters of this book.

'Go with the flow'

You remember that the advice of the last wizard was: 'Your trouble, my son, is that you have been trying to resist life instead of surrendering to it. Forget all this stuff the other wizards have been telling you. Just go with the flow. Let life take you where it will. Live for the moment. Follow the path of least resistance.'

His advice to Hans to go with the flow represents a radically different approach to time-management from the methods the other wizards gave and which I have been describing up to now in this chapter. In fact it could really almost be called an anti-time-management method. It has such different characteristics that it is not generally to be found in the same category of books as the other advice. Rather than appearing in books about time-management it tends to be found in books on spirituality. As the wizard said, the root concept is that instead of trying to *manage* life we should *surrender* to it. If we do that, so the theory goes, we will find the way opening up in front of us and will have no need to fuss and fret ourselves trying to manage the unmanageable.

The problem with going with the flow is that most of us do not have a firm enough structure to make our lives flow properly. An apt metaphor here is the difference between a swamp and a river. They are both made of water, but the difference is that the river has banks and is going somewhere while a swamp has no banks and is going nowhere. When most people attempt to go with the flow all that happens is that they get stuck in the swamp. They try to follow the path of least resistance but, since a swamp provides no resistance, all that happens is that we stagnate.

What we need in order to be able to go with the flow is adequate banks for our river to provide the resistance to make the waters of our life flow. This is a subject I shall be exploring in the last chapters of this book where I shall be bringing the two radically different methods of time-management into a synthesis. Our aim is always to be able to flow into doing the right things at the right time. But we have still a lot of ground to cover before we get there.

We have spent this chapter examining most of the currently accepted advice on time-management to see what its uses and limitations are. On the way we have discovered that none of it is really suitable for lifting the majority of people out of the impasse they find themselves in.

In the next chapter we will look at what is needed to provide a system which will really enable people to manage their lives in the way they want.

Action summary

- Use prioritising in an emergency or when you have to meet an urgent deadline.
- Use 'Do it now' to keep you on track when carrying out routines and predetermined tasks.
- When a problem occurs, direct your attention to *why* the problem occurred.

- Write checklists to break down the action needed for a project or to ensure that a task is completed properly.
- Write programmes to co-ordinate your actions with those of another person or persons.
- Remember that to go with the flow, you need to have some banks for your river!

5

What We Need in a Time- and Life-Management System

As we have seen in the last chapter, it is not enough to provide good-sounding techniques which will in reality only help people in some specific circumstances. We need the keys which will enable us to make a radical transformation in our whole way of living. In this chapter we will be looking at what we would need in a really effective system of life-management. In particular we will be looking in more detail at the subject which is the root cause of most time- and life-management problems – resistance.

Sufficient regular focused attention is the key to success

It is a pretty good rule of thumb in life that our circumstances reflect what we have been paying attention to. If we have paid attention to our fitness, we will have a high standard of fitness. If we pay attention to our work, we will have a high standard of work. If we pay attention to our marriage, we will have a high standard of marriage. I don't mean that we will escape all difficulties, setbacks or failures. On the contrary there may even be more of these because we are more willing to take risks and undertake new ventures. But if we are in the habit of giving matters the attention they need, we will be equipped to deal with difficulties as they arise.

On the other hand, if we give our full attention only to what is on the television we may have a good knowledge of television trivia but not much else to show for it. Or if our attention is dispersed without being focused on any one thing for long, then our lives will reflect that by being chaotic and aimless.

The human brain is remarkably efficient at filtering the mass of information we are presented with so that it presents us with what is relevant to what we are paying attention to at the time. You may have remarked that when you buy a new car you suddenly start noticing every time you drive past a car of the same make and model. You don't have to be looking out for them, your brain presents them to you automatically.

Whenever we pay attention to something, the incredible powers of our brains are unleashed. Almost any problem or challenge can be solved by our attention. Sadly most people's attention is diffused, fragmented and wasted on trivial matters. One of my aims in this book is to show you that this does not have to be the case.

However, to say that our attention can solve virtually any problem is not quite enough. There are several conditions that need to be met.

Attention needs to be focused

An attention that is leaping back and forth between one subject and another, that is continually being distracted or withdrawn as soon as it encounters resistance, is not sufficient. Attention must be focused to be effective.

It needs to be regular

Anything that does not get regular attention will start to change for the worse. This applies to our houseplants, our gardens, our cars, our work, our families, our health and indeed everything in our lives. If attention is only spasmodic then the results will be only spasmodic at best.

It needs to be sufficient

However regular and focused our attention may be, it will not achieve the results we want unless it is sufficient. If a project is given insufficient attention then we lose out on two counts – first, we will not achieve our aims for that project and, second, we will have wasted attention that we could have used to forward some other project. In our discussion about prioritisation in the last chapter, I stressed the pointlessness of having *anything* in our lives to which we are not able to give sufficient attention.

I often get into a conversation like this with people who come to me for advice:

'I want to learn how to prioritise my work better.'

'What exactly do you mean by that?'

'I mean I want to know which things to spend time on and which things to spend less time on.'

'You mean you want to know which things to do well and which things to do badly?'

The reason most projects fail is that they are not given sufficient regular focused attention. The reason projects succeed is that they *are* given sufficient regular focused attention. This applies just as much to keeping our back garden in good order as to a huge civil engineering project. Our system of life-management must ensure this sufficient, regular, focused attention for all our projects or it will be worthless.

Resistance and procrastination are the biggest life-management problems

Resistance is at the root of virtually every life-management problem. By this I mean the resistance that we put up to what is happening in our lives. One very damaging result of resistance is procrastination. This can come in some very subtle forms. For example, busyness is a subtle form of procrastination in which we fill our lives with activity to avoid doing what really needs doing.

Essentially resistance happens when one activity is harder for us than another one. By this I mean subjectively rather than objectively harder. An activity may be technically difficult but it is nevertheless easy for us to concentrate on it because we enjoy it or are committed to it. Something that is considerably easier in technique may create more resistance within us and therefore be psychologically far more difficult for us to do. A good example of this would be a concert pianist who finds it easy to play the piano but incredibly difficult to sort out her tax return.

Resistance is the reason that our lives tend to fill up with trivia. There is no unalterable law that they must. But the fact is that dealing with trivia is *easier* than dealing with important issues.

One of the laws of resistance is that the more we avoid something the greater the resistance becomes. Therefore every time we put something off, the more difficult it becomes to do. It would be nice if resistance then went away for a bit and left us alone – but it does not. It remains present as a cloud of unspecified anxiety.

Fortunately the reverse is true. When we do succeed in overcoming our resistance and get going on something, it becomes easier to do. In fact once something has been begun, a resistance to stopping doing it may start to build up. This too can cause problems. We can get so carried away by an activity that we do it to the exclusion of everything else.

Another law of resistance is that once resistance builds up beyond a certain level we find ourselves literally unable to do a task. This threshold is different for different people, and the aim of several of the exercises in this book is to increase your resistance threshold. We remain unable to do the task until the penalty for not doing it becomes sufficiently unpleasant. In other words until the pain of not doing it becomes greater than the pain of doing it. If we have been putting something off for a long time this can involve a very high level of pain indeed.

Our life-management system needs to give us a method of overcoming resistance. In fact this needs to be its primary focus, otherwise our resistance will always succeed in sabotaging us in spite of all our goals and plans and hopes and dreams.

The problem with virtually all systems for managing our time is that they do not give sufficient importance to the overcoming of resistance.

A system should be in place for dealing with every bit of work that presents itself

Whatever form of life-management system we have, it must be capable of dealing with every task that presents itself. What I mean by this is that there is no point having a system that can deal efficiently with the post that arrives once a day but is thrown by e-mail that arrives throughout the day. Or that cannot cope if we move from one place of work to another. Our system needs to be able to cope with every sort of eventuality so that we don't have to invent the system as we go along.

Good systems are essential for efficient work. The time spent in designing a system will be saved many times over every day that it is in place. But often, in spite of the irritation caused by a bad or non-existent system, it is just too much trouble or we

Table 1: A method of overcoming resistance
The symptoms of resistance
• Procrastination
• Time taken up with trivia and 'easy work'
• Interruptions allowed to distract
• Dispersed attention
• Unfocused anxiety
• Frequent crises and emergencies
• Refusal to delegate
The laws of resistance
• Resistance is increased when something is avoided.
• Resistance is decreased when something is actioned.
• Once a certain level of resistance has been reached ('the resistance threshold') it becomes virtually impossible to do a task.
• Beyond the resistance threshold we will only do a task once the pain of not doing it becomes greater than the pain of doing it.
How to overcome resistance
• Take action before resistance builds up.
• Break large tasks down into smaller steps.
• Increase the pain of not doing it.
• Get resistance working *for* you by setting up good routines and systems to 'automate' as many tasks as possible.

haven't got time to work out a better one. So we carry on month after month or year after year working at less than our full potential. Again until the pain caused by the faulty system becomes greater than the pain of putting it right, nothing will be done.

So it is with a time-management system – it must not be causing us aggravation or we will have a continual undercurrent of tension that will never be quite bad enough to do anything about. The essential point about a system that works well is that it never draws attention to itself. If you have to think about what to do with a piece of work that presents itself, then it is likely to get put aside and forgotten about.

Another reason for spending time setting up good systems is that once you have been adhering to them for a while they become automatic or 'second nature', as we say. A good example of this is putting your seat belt on when you get in a car. If you frequently fail to put it on, then it becomes a bother to put it on, and you will continue to wear it only intermittently. If you make yourself put it on every time, then in a week or so it becomes so much second nature that you don't even consciously notice that you've done it. The same applies to all good systems and routines. It may take time and effort to set them up, but once they are up and running and we make ourselves adhere to them they become automatic and greatly reduce the mental effort that goes into our work. We will be looking further at the implication of this in the final chapters of this book.

Much of the difficulty we have in managing our lives is caused by bad systems and routines which continually produce problems, but never quite enough to force us to change them. (Remember that by and large we will only change something if the pain of continuing to do it becomes greater than the pain of changing it.) Often the secret of breaking the bad habit is to increase the pain artificially. For example, if you are giving up smoking you can adapt an old remedy to a new use by setting yourself a rule that every time you light a cigarette you have to go and take a cold shower.

You do not have to go to quite these lengths to change simple work routines but the same principle applies. I had a problem changing my working practices when my computer was upgraded to a new operating system. Under the old operating system when I closed a program the memory used by that program was released. Under the new operating system it was not released. I persisted in closing programs in the new system as I had done in the old one – with the result that my computer would gradually grind to a halt as reopened programs demanded more and more memory. Don't worry about the details of this if you are not a computer expert – the point is that the new system required precisely the opposite action to the old system and I couldn't break myself of the habit of doing it the old way. Finally I hit on the idea of making myself reboot the computer every time I took the wrong action. This served a double purpose. First, it recovered the memory my action had forfeited and, second, it was such a tedious process that I very quickly abandoned my faulty action.

Exercise

Identify a bad work habit you have. Make it a simple one like not putting books and files away when you have finished with them. Give yourself a penalty for not doing it. It might be something on the lines of whenever you find a book or file which you have not put away, you have to put it away by a circuitous route involving a couple of flights of stairs. That way you get to be tidy and take exercise at the same time!

Another characteristic of good systems and routines is that once they have been established they cause considerable resistance if we *don't* do them. This has important implications for keeping us on the right track. You will remember from our earlier discussion that if we want to 'go with the flow' then we need to be like a river which has banks to produce resistance. Otherwise there will be no flow; we shall instead stay in the same place and stagnate.

The ability to cope with interruptions and emergencies is essential

If we invest some time and thought in setting up good systems, we should eventually find that we have fewer interruptions to our work – but it is too much to hope that we will never have any at all. We have already seen how scheduling is particularly vulnerable to interruptions. Leaving ourselves vulnerable to interruptions may also be a subtle form of procrastination – it is easier to deal with an interruption than to deal with what we should be working on. The same applies to continuous crises and emergencies. 'Troubleshooting' can be a very useful way of persuading oneself that one is acting decisively and effectively without having to face up to the question of why there is so much trouble to shoot in the first place.

So our system must be able to flow round interruptions and emergencies whilst at the same time encouraging us to take the measures that will reduce their number.

Action summary

- The key to success is attention that is
  - sufficient;
  - regular;
  - focused.
- The more we avoid doing something the greater our resistance to doing it becomes.
- When we get going on something it becomes easier to keep working on it.
- Break bad habits by making the pain of doing them greater than the pain of not doing them.
- Set up good systems to automate your life and free up time to be creative.

6

The Different Types
of Tasks

Before I start to integrate what we have discussed so far into a
workable system, I want to spend a chapter looking at the
different types of task we may be faced with. Basically we can
classify every task according one of three types, each of which
requires to be handled in a different way. One of the keys to
managing our life is to know and appreciate the characteristics
of each of these.

These three types are:

* tasks that come with a time attached;
* tasks that should have a time attached;
* tasks that do not have a time attached.

The first place to look if you want more time is items with a time attached

Many tasks come with a time attached. By this I mean such things as meetings, appointments, performances, mealtimes, picking up children from school, TV programmes, cinema showings and so on. There is an immense variety of possible tasks that can fall into this category but they all tend to share similar characteristics.

First, they almost invariably involve other people. The reason they have a time attached is *because* they involve other people. If they didn't involve other people they wouldn't need a time attached.

Second, the time is critical. We either succeed in being on time or suffer the consequences of not being on time. In some cases this may matter very little, in others there may be serious consequences. But there is always a progression by which 'early' turns to 'on time' and then to 'late'. It is a fact often remarked that people have a strong tendency to run always at about the same degree of earliness or lateness. If you are habitually five minutes late you will tend to be about five minutes late for everything, whatever the degree of importance. And similarly some people can be relied upon to be five minutes early for everything.

Apart from our own place on the early/late scale we are also dependent on other people. If other people are late that wastes our time; if we are late that wastes other people's time. We have lost control of our own attention and are dependent on others. Even worse, the start-time may be reasonably within our control, but the end-time may be completely out of our hands. A committee meeting may drag on for much longer than we were expecting, a seminar may finish late, the appointment with our boss takes twice as long as we allowed for. It is out of our hands.

Which brings me on to the most important characteristic of these items. They usually take up much more of our time than would appear at first glance. A half-hour meeting one morning may hardly seem to make much of a hole in our diaries. But if we have to travel for thirty minutes to get there, wait around for ten minutes for everyone to arrive and the meeting then finishes twenty minutes late, we have lost two hours out of our morning, not counting preparation time. And if we then say 'It's not worth starting anything else before lunch' we have lost a whole morning's work for the sake of one short meeting.

So if you want to find more time in your life, the first place to look is at these items. Of course I am not suggesting that we can or should get rid of all appointments and meetings, but that we must be very careful to ensure that we are getting sufficient value out of them. If a meeting takes three hours of our attention, are we getting three hours' worth of value out of it? Again and again we must remind ourselves that our attention is a valuable commodity and a limited one too.

Exercise

Work out how much time you spent in total on all the meetings that you had scheduled last week. Include all the time you spent on preparation, travel and recovery – all the time in fact that you could have spent on something else if you had not attended that meeting.

Then when you have done this, cost out each meeting in the way suggested earlier in this book. If you haven't already put a monetary value on your attention, then work out now what the value of one hour of your attention is to you. So if you put a value of £15 an hour on your time, a meeting that takes up three hours of your attention will be costed at £45.

Ask yourself 'Would I have been willing to pay £45 for what I got out of that meeting?' Even if the answer is 'Yes', you can ask yourself the additional question 'Could I have achieved the same result for less cost?'

Then have a look at what the total cost to you in time and money is of all the meetings you attended that week. If you are like most of us, you may see clearly for the first time what the true effects of filling your diary with appointments are. Some of these will be well worth the cost, others will most definitely not be. One of the key life-management skills is to be able to distinguish which are worthwhile and which are not, and to decline to be involved in those that are not.

Case study – planned-giving campaigns

My own experience in the world of Christian stewardship provides a useful example of how looking clearly at the necessity of meetings can transform the effectiveness of one's work. In 1989 I was given the task of running planned giving campaigns within the Diocese of Chichester. This is a diocese of the Church of England that covers the whole of East and West Sussex and contains some two hundred and fifty parishes. The aim of a planned-giving campaign is to give the members of a church's congregation a clear picture of the church's finances and to ask them to respond by pledging to give a regular amount either weekly or monthly, either by banker's order or by putting an envelope containing their giving into the collection plate.

When I took over the job, the standard method of doing this was known as a Christian Stewardship campaign. This could be a very effective way of obtaining the results but was very labour intensive. As commonly practised, it would involve the adviser in at least eight visits to the parish over a period of some six months, plus a lot of work by the members of the parish themselves. Most of the adviser's visits had to take place in the evening as that was usually the only time that the members of a church could get together.

There was quite a lot of rationalisation about what these meetings were achieving. It was felt that parishes could not be trusted to get on with the planning process themselves, that the adviser needed to get to know the parish well if he or she were to be appreciated by them, and that the parish would expect the adviser to be present at all meetings and would not think he was doing his job if he were not. To me, these reasons seemed to have more to do with the adviser's own needs than with the needs of the task.

What seemed to have escaped most people's attention was that it was all very well for the adviser to be seen to be doing his job 'properly', but if eight or more evening visits were required by an adviser to a parish, then that severely limited the number of campaigns in which that adviser could be involved. A reasonable assumption would be that an adviser would not be able to dedicate more than three evenings a week to these campaigns. Simple mathematics will then tell you that each adviser would be physically unable to run more than one campaign every three weeks. Allowing for holidays, the effect of major church festivals and other factors, that probably means that each adviser would have an upper limit of about fourteen campaigns a year.

It struck me immediately that if it were possible to get the number of evening meetings down to three, then the adviser would be able to cope with one campaign a week. As the only adviser in my diocese, I would need to be able to work at this sort of rate if I was going to be able to make any sort of real impact. I decided that I needed a simpler type of campaign which would mean that the parishes could cope with most of the planning themselves without needing constant input from me.

The simpler form of campaign allowed me to move the main presentation so that it took place during the normal Sunday service, instead of having it as part of a major function on a weekday evening. This had the advantage that a large proportion of the potential audience would be going to church anyway on a Sunday. Also, since I too would normally be going to church on a Sunday morning, it did not take up any of my own time that I wouldn't anyway have spent in church. I then reduced the evening meetings during the week to three – an introductory meeting at which I explained the concept to the church council, a planning meeting and a training meeting. I always left it open to the parish that they could ask me to make further visits if they needed them, but not once did I need to be taken up on this. All difficulties could be – and were – quite satisfactorily sorted out on the telephone.

In one year (1993) I actually succeeded in running forty-eight campaigns as a result of these changes. Each campaign was raising the level of planned giving in the parish concerned by an average of 65 per cent. In the space of just over two years, we succeeded in raising pledged annual giving by £1 million. This vast improvement in productivity happened simply because I'd asked myself the question: 'What are these meetings actually achieving?'

Depth activities need to have a time attached or they will be shunted aside

I have already mentioned that one of the problems of modern life is that we have exchanged depth for width. We tend to get involved in more and more things in a shallower and shallower way. In earlier centuries life might have been far more constricted, even for the rich and powerful, but it was lived in a less shallow way. Tradition and local culture were not to be found in museums or put on show for tourists but formed the very fabric of life and provided a depth of experience and community that is unknown to us today.

It is neither possible nor desirable for us to attempt to regress to the experiences of an earlier age. But we can become more deeply involved in our experience of the present. Such activities as prayer, meditation, journal-writing and the like can help to deepen our lives. We may have other activities that we wish to carry out on a regular basis, such as studying or exercise. These are all things that take us away from the daily grind of clashing priorities and help to provide an oasis of calm. When we succeed in doing them, the rest of the day usually feels right. When we fail to do them the day often seems to have been put out of kilter.

The problem with activities of this type, which I call 'depth activities', is that they are usually the first to go when we feel harassed or short of time. Of course it is precisely in these circumstances that we need them most. And once we have lost the habit of doing them, then they will get done more and more rarely.

The best way to do this type of regular, recurring, daily activity is to schedule a specific time for it each day which is inviolate. You need to decide for yourself what your best time is. For many people – myself included – it is first thing in the morning before doing anything else. Whether your 'depth activity' is prayer or jogging or writing, it needs to be started immediately you rise from bed – before you get dressed, make a cup of coffee or clean your teeth. Once you start doing something else, you are lost – the pressures of the world will start closing in on you and you will never get back to your depth activity.

Another good time is immediately after returning home from work so that you are set up for the rest of the evening. Again it is important to get moving on the depth activity before you start getting involved in anything else.

I want to sound a note of warning here: it is very difficult to keep to this type of activity on a consistent basis. So you need to give yourself as good a framework as possible to help yourself. One way of ensuring you will not succeed in keeping to your depth activities is to have too many. If you are doing a full day's work and suddenly decide that you are going to meditate *and* do yoga *and* go for a run *and* learn a foreign language, you will be setting yourself up to fail – with the result that after a few days or weeks you will be doing none of them. If you do want to do more than one, then introduce them into your life one at a time and make sure that each one is properly established before introducing the next. Remember: better to do a few things well than many things badly.

Depth activities are very helpful to us in giving us the right mindset to manage our lives in the way we want to. In the final chapter of this book I will be looking in more detail at some of them and how they can help us in this respect.

Exercise

If you don't already have at least one depth activity which you are doing on a regular basis, then why not decide on one right now? Perhaps it will be something new; perhaps it will be something you used to do and don't any longer. If you need some suggestions, read the final chapter of this book where several are discussed. Your activity can be whatever you like – the important things are that it should be something you can do every day and that you should feel better for doing it. Then decide what the optimum time for doing it would be and block out that time in your schedule. Regard it as an appointment with yourself which is every bit as important as an appointment with a client or your boss.

How you deal with free-flowing activities is the key to good time-management

All other items – those which don't have a time attached – are what I call 'free-flowing' activities. By this I mean that they are like the water in a river that flows freely round the rocks – rocks which are made up of the scheduled items in our day.

Free-flowing items may have a deadline sometime in the future, but until that deadline it is up to you how and when you action them. This has the great advantage of giving freedom and flexibility to these items. But also at the same time it gives more opportunity to the danger of procrastination and resistance building up.

Without the structure which a scheduled time imposes on us, free-floating items are difficult to control, and this is exacerbated by the fact that they usually include most of the actions to which we have the highest resistance.

So if free-flowing items are dealt with badly they have the maximum potential for disrupting our lives. If we can control them, then we will have the ability to run our lives in a flexible and responsive way that accords with our real needs as they arise.

Good time-management depends more than anything else on how well we manage these free-flowing items. In the next chapter I will be putting forward some techniques which will enable you to get these free-flowing items under control immediately. But remember the point I have made several times already in this book: no techniques can enable you to cram a quart into a pint pot. If you have not examined your activities by working through the earlier exercises which I have given, all you are likely to succeed in doing is to process trivia more efficiently.

Remember that our tendency is to concentrate on easy trivial items at the expense of more difficult and more important items. It is not difficult to identify if this is happening to you. Just ask yourself two questions: 'Am I being overwhelmed by the quantity of work I have?' 'Does the work I am actually succeeding in doing stretch me mentally?' If your answer to the first question is 'Yes' and to the second question 'No', then you are probably using busyness as an escape from challenging yourself. Ideally our work should be stretching but not overwhelming. The more you stretch yourself mentally, the less you will be overwhelmed with trivia – for the very good reason that you won't need it any more. And most important of all, the more you stretch yourself the easier you will find it to get into the flow state where everything seems to happen almost of itself.

John

John is a senior marketing executive in a medium-sized engineering firm. He is married with young children, and when he came to me his marriage had been under stress for some time. The reason he gave was that he had a high-pressure job and, although the money was good, he was becoming more and more unhappy with the way his work was taking up the whole of his life. He felt that he was becoming 'a work machine' and all of his life outside work was suffering.

When we examined together the way in which his day was

made up, it became increasingly obvious that he had got himself into a vicious circle. His former genuine interest and absorption in his work had caused resentment from his wife, who felt reasonably enough that she and her children were being neglected. But instead of facing up to this situation and doing something about it, he had attempted to avoid the problem at home by taking on yet more work so that he could spend less time in what was becoming an unfriendly home environment.

It was vital to break the vicious circle, so I advised him to set a rigid time each day after which he would not work but would go home. I also advised him to take an audit of all the work meetings in which he was involved in order to cut out the ones that were not totally necessary. I asked him to look particularly at situations where individual phone calls, conference calls or e-mail could be as effective as a face-to-face meeting with a much smaller time penalty. I also encouraged him to take up some form of daily exercise before work and fifteen minutes' writing in a journal in the evening. These would help him to balance his life better and get him away from the feeling that life was all work.

He reported back that in spite of the shorter hours his effectiveness at work had actually improved. Journal-writing had helped him to work out some of his feelings about his wife, and he had eventually found himself able to discuss these with her for the first time. Their relationship had considerably improved and, rather than feeling desperate about life as a whole, he had now regained positive feelings about both his work and his marriage.

Action summary

- Always ask yourself how much value a meeting or scheduled appointment is going to contribute before you commit yourself to it.
- Your life needs depth activities to keep it in balance.

- Introduce depth activities into your life one at a time and get each one established before you introduce another.
- Don't fill your time with 'easy work'. It's the challenging work which will achieve your goals.

7

How to Deal with Free-Flowing Items

In this chapter I will be giving you several techniques for dealing with free-flowing items. Each one of them is valuable in its own right, but I will also be showing you an example of how to put them together into an integrated system which will fulfil all of the conditions I mentioned in the previous chapter. The system I shall be showing you is suitable as a starting point, but as you gain practice in improving your ability to organise yourself you may find that you outgrow it. In any case it is not intended to be followed rigidly but made the basis for making your own refinements. When running seminars on time-management, I always advise the participants to regard it as the default settings on a computer, which you can alter to fit your own preferences. In the following chapter, I will be looking further at how you can tailor-make your own system to suit your own needs and style of working.

Working in short bursts is the key to overcoming resistance

Before you read any further, I want you do another exercise. For this you will need a timer of some kind, a pen or pencil and a few sheets of paper, preferably lined.

Exercise

First of all I want you to select an issue or a problem in your life to which you know you need to give some serious thought but have been putting off doing so. It does not matter what the issue is, business or personal. All that matters is that you have been avoiding thinking about it in a focused way.

Now I want you to read to the end of these instructions before putting them into effect. The aim is to write about the subject for five minutes without stopping. And when I say 'without stopping' I mean it literally. Don't stop to think – don't go back over what you have written – don't worry about punctuation, spelling or grammar. Keep your hand moving. When the five minutes is up, stop dead.

Set your timer. Start your writing now and stop the second the timer goes off.

When you have finished, read through what you have written and underline anything you feel is particularly significant – such as a new insight or some action to be taken. Then write down everything you have underlined as a separate list.

Most people are surprised how many insights they get through doing this exercise. In a mere five minutes' concentrated writing they often come up with new angles that might have taken them days or weeks to think of otherwise.

I have given you this exercise for two reasons. First because it is a useful tool in its own right for obtaining insights about any issue. Add it to your repertoire of creative methods. Of course it doesn't have to be five minutes that you write for – it can be any length of time – but the important thing is that you write non-stop for a defined period.

The second reason is to show you how much you can accomplish in five minutes. If you are like most people who try this exercise you have probably got further with your chosen issue during this five-minute exercise than you have in the previous few weeks or even months.

Now what do you think would have happened if I had said that I wanted you to write about the issue for *at least* five minutes, rather than *exactly* five minutes? You may feel that you could have explored the subject more deeply, but the experience of most people is the opposite – working for an undefined period of time is not as effective as working for a defined period of time. Having a definite cut-off time concentrates the mind.

I call this the 'end-effect'. Our most effective work is usually done at the end of a time period, particularly when there is a very definite cut-off point. We all know the Friday-afternoon syndrome, when everyone clears their desk before the weekend. Think too of what happens just before you go on holiday. You probably clear more work in the last couple of days than you succeeded in doing in the previous two weeks. Both these are examples of the end-effect applied to a long period of a week or more. But it is quite possible to build the end-effect into our lives on a more consistent basis by using much shorter time periods. In a moment we will be exploring how to do this.

The corollary is that if we do not build in the end-effect, our work will lack concentration. If you are someone who regularly works through lunch or stays late at the office, you may not be doing any more work than the person who stops dead at the official stopping time. The reason is because you are depriving yourself of end-effects.

This is often a major problem with people who work at home. Because their work and their personal life tend to run into each other, they don't have any natural end-effects built into their day. This results in their work lacking focus and concentration.

So the five-minute writing exercise you have just done is a fine example of the end-effect in action. Because there is a definite cut-off at five minutes we are achieving on a small scale the same sort of result as clearing our desk before going on holiday.

But the five-minute exercise also illustrates another important principle. I deliberately asked you to write about a subject which you had been putting off considering – in other words a subject that you have had some degree of resistance about starting. You were probably wondering when you had finished the exercise why you had been resisting it so much in the first place. In fact now you may be keen to get moving on some of the insights that came to you – perhaps you even rushed off and did some of them before continuing to read this chapter.

The reason for this is that a short burst is an extremely effective way of overcoming resistance. It is probably true to say that anyone can work at *anything* for five minutes. And even if you only succeed in getting the file out or looking up a telephone number, you will have begun to get yourself moving. And once you have started moving, much of the resistance will start to fall away. Our natural inertia is what prevents us from getting going, but it is also what keeps us going once we have started something. Once you have expended effort in overcoming the resistance that keeps you paralysed, you have started to build momentum. For this reason there is a lot of truth in the old adage that the best antidote for fear is action.

There is another very significant advantage of stopping dead at the end of a short burst of work. The human mind craves completion and you will be left with the feeling that you have not finished the task and want to get on with it. If you then come back to it after a reasonable interval, you will find that your mind has been working on it subconsciously in the meantime. Your ideas will have progressed further than they would have if you had continued working without a break.

So, to summarise, short timed bursts are excellent for over-coming resistance to a task – they produce a concentrated work flow and leave you raring to get going again.

Exercise

Try the following experiment. Work at a fairly routine job, such as processing your correspondence or your e-mail, in ten-minute bursts. Do three bursts of ten minutes, with a gap of a few minutes between each burst. Don't forget to stop dead as soon as each ten-minute period is up.

When you've done the three sessions of ten minutes each, compare how much work you've managed to do with how much you'd normally expect to do in thirty minutes of continuous untimed work. You will probably find not only that you have dealt with considerably more work but that the whole process has seemed much easier and more relaxed and your attention has wandered less.

Bursts should be lengthened as momentum builds up

Five- or ten-minute bursts may be very effective in getting us started, but we would obviously drive ourselves crazy if we were to live our whole lives in a series of bursts of a few minutes. So as we get going on a subject and build up some momentum we can lengthen the burst.

I suggest you begin by adding five minutes to the length of the burst each time. So you would first do a five-minute burst, then a ten-minute one, then fifteen minutes, twenty minutes and so on. I would not lengthen the bursts beyond forty minutes as that is about the maximum that you can work intensely without losing concentration, but in any case it is only relatively rarely that you ever need to build up to that length of burst. If you do occasionally find that you need to do more work, then continue doing forty-minute bursts without increasing further.

You can go on doing this until you find you have lost momentum. This usually happens after a longer than usual gap between bursts. A good rule is that whenever you feel you have lost momentum, shorten the length of the bursts – if necessary right back to five minutes – and then start increasing the length again.

Rotating systematically round a list of categories ensures all areas of work are covered

I've been talking about using bursts of increasing lengths with gaps in between. There is no reason why gaps have to be limited to a couple of minutes – they can be much longer than that. You can then take advantage of the gaps to work in the same way on another subject. So you might do something like this. Work on Project A for five minutes, then Project B for five minutes. Then go back to Project A and work for ten minutes and then Project B for ten minutes. Then both in turn for fifteen minutes, then twenty minutes.

By doing this you will have worked in a concentrated way for a total of an hour and forty minutes on two subjects, taking full advantage of the end-effect. You will find that there is an unbelievable difference between what you have just achieved and what you would normally expect to get through in that length of time.

You may ask: 'What happens if I get interrupted – does an interruption throw this method of working out?' The answer is 'No!' All you have to do is deal with the interruption and then go back to where you were in the burst. If you are using a kitchen-timer, for example, it is easy enough to glance at the timer when the interruption starts and then once it is over to set the timer back to where it was. Or if you want to be less scientific, just estimate how far in the burst you had got.

Exercise

Take two subjects and try out the method I have just outlined.
Do them in turn, increasing the length of time you work on them
each time. You can use any subjects you like, but you may find it
best not to make them too similar and to make at least one of
them a subject you have been putting off. So you might alternate
dealing with your e-mail with sorting out your filing system, or
writing a course project with tidying your office. It doesn't matter
what you choose, so long as you do it!

Now you have tried this method with two subjects you do not
have to stop there. You can increase the number of subjects to
well beyond two. I have frequently used as many as ten or more
items on my list. This works surprisingly well since many of the
items will be dealt with completely during the ten-minute burst
or even sometimes during the five-minute burst. The list then
narrows down to concentrate on those items that need more time.
Often by the time one has got to twenty-minute bursts there are
only two or three items on the list.

This is a powerful way of working because the constant variety
of items keeps the mind fresh. And you are getting moving on all
your outstanding work – which helps to stop you worrying about
all the things you are *not* doing.

Using checklists rather than individual items allows work to be done in context

I mentioned in an earlier chapter that I do not like to-do lists. A
to-do list is a list of out-of-context items and has a natural
tendency to proliferation. A checklist by contrast shows what is
needed to achieve a project or task and the more items you have
on it the better the task will be completed.

It makes sense, therefore, to work from a series of checklists
rather than from a to-do list. Draw up a list consisting first of all

of the routine items that need to be handled every day, such as e-mail, letters, telephone, filing, tidying, accounts etc. Then add to this list the various projects that you are involved in. What these are will be specific to your particular work, but for someone who runs their own business it might include things like Client Follow Up, Prospecting, Publicity, Move to New Premises etc.

Taking these together, your complete list might read:

e-mail
letters
phone
filing
accounts
client follow up
prospecting
publicity
new premises

To begin with, at least, aim to keep the list to no more than ten items. You can now rotate round this list in the way I have suggested. For each project you will be working off a checklist. In this way you will ensure that you are giving your project focused attention. I will be giving more advice on how to make checklists in the next chapter.

You can use bursts for rest periods as well

Just as a short timed work period can be more concentrated than a work period of unspecified length, so a short timed rest period can be more relaxing than a longer period without a specific ending time. Try the experiment of breaking up your work with timed rest periods of five minutes during which you do whatever comes into your mind. You can make yourself a cup of coffee, read the newspaper, talk to a friend, take a nap, get some fresh air, or even do a few odd jobs – but the point is that you are letting your attention freewheel for a few minutes. This will rest your attention and make it easier to concentrate when you get back to work. But remember – you must get back to work the second the timer goes off!

Putting these principles together results in a powerful system for dealing with free-flowing items

Now what we have been describing is the heart of my method for dealing with free-flowing items. But here I want to repeat my earlier warning. If you are still trying to cram too much into your life, all you will succeed in doing is processing trivia more efficiently. But if you have gone through the exercise of reviewing your commitments so that you have sufficient attention available for everything, then you will start to make some real advances.

So, to recap, draw up a list of routine activities and projects. Be ruthless in not allowing this to grow beyond ten items until you are well established in the system. Start a checklist for each of the projects (you can do this in the first five-minute burst). Then rotate round the list, increasing the intervals. As you do each one cross out the length of burst you have just done and put in the next length, e.g.

e-mail	5	10
letters	5	
phone	5	
filing	5	
tidy	5	
accounts	5	
client follow up	5	
prospecting	5	
publicity	5	
new premises	5	

Whenever you succeed in finishing an item or going as far as you wish to go with it at that time, then start again from the beginning of the series. So if you managed for example to finish all outstanding phone calls in five minutes or less, put 5 instead of 10 as the next interval, e.g.

e-mail	~~5~~	10
letters	~~5~~	10
phone	~~5~~	5
etc.		

Now once you have been running the list for some time, the different items will have a variety of different lengths of burst.

Let's see how this might work out in practice.

First Step

You draw up your list of items and allocate five minutes to each item:

e-mail	5
letters	5
phone	5
filing	5
tidy	5
accounts	5
client follow up	5
prospecting	5
publicity	5
new premises	5

You work through the list, doing five minutes on each item. You cross out the 5 against that item as you finish it. If everything has been finished under that item, put a 5 for the next pass. If you still have work to do then increase the length to 10 for the next burst, like this:

e-mail	5	10
letters	5	5
phone	5	5
filing	5	10
tidy	5	5
accounts	5	10
client follow up	5	10
prospecting	5	10
publicity	5	10
new premises	5	10

In this example, there was little or nothing to do under the headings Letters, Phone and Tidy, so you successfully completed them in five minutes. Consequently you put them down as having five minutes available in the next pass. Everything else did not get completed so you put them down for ten minutes in the next pass.

Now let's look what might happen the next time through:

e-mail	5	~~10~~	5
letters	5	5	5
phone	5	5	10
filing	5	~~10~~	5
tidy	5	5	5
accounts	5	~~10~~	15
client follow up	5	~~10~~	15
prospecting	5	~~10~~	15
publicity	5	~~10~~	15
new premises	5	~~10~~	15

This time we finished E-mail so it reverts to five minutes next time. There was nothing new under Letters so it remained at five. But several new phone messages had come in and could not be completed in five minutes, so the time interval is increased to ten. Filing is completed so reverts to five and any tidying to be done took less than five minutes so remains at five for the next time round. The five final items all have outstanding work, so they are increased to fifteen minutes.

Some tips for making the system work

1 Be strict with yourself about cutting off working on a subject when the time is up. If you carry on working you will lose the benefit of the end-effect and will start to drift. Of course if you start something that can't be interrupted like a phone call or a trip to the local shop, you finish it. But remember to get back to the next item as soon as possible.

2 Always start the next item immediately. Set your timer for the next item as soon as it goes off for the previous item. If you don't do this, you will get distracted in the gaps between items. And, before you know it, the gaps will become longer than the work times.

3 Give yourself a limited target for each item. So if one of your items is writing a book, give yourself a target of writing so many pages or revising one chapter. Once you have achieved that target, set the interval back to five and start a new target. Otherwise you will be spending too long on one subject to the detriment of others.

4 Don't have too many items on your list. There is no quicker way to kill this system than to attempt to use it to do too much. In a later chapter I will be looking at ways in which you can vary your work over the different days of a week.

5 Make sure the subjects you put on your list cover the whole of your work. You don't want items coming up which can't immediately find a place on your list. Everything that doesn't fit into the system will get neglected.

6 Give yourself regular timed breaks. A five-minute break every thirty minutes or so makes a lot of difference to how tiring work is. Do anything you like during the break, but make sure you start working again as soon as it is up.

7 Never take a break when you have finished something. Always start the next thing first, and then take the break. We have

mentioned the reason for this before. The human mind craves completion. If you take a break when you have finished something, your mind has registered that you have finished and it is difficult to get back to work. But if you stop dead while still working on something, your mind wants to get back to work to finish it.

Exercise

1 Draw up a list of up to ten subjects. A good way of doing this is to list everything that you have done over the last couple of weeks plus everything you have outstanding, and then group them. Make sure that all items are contained in a group. Divide groups up and amalgamate them until you have the right number. Don't worry too much about getting this grouping exactly right – you can keep revising your list of groups as you work on them.

2 Now set yourself a target for today in respect of each item on your list. In some cases it may be to complete all outstanding work, e.g. deal with all today's e-mail. In others it may be limited, e.g. write five pages of your book, plan the layout for next month's newsletter or read a long magazine article.

3 Now rotate the list in the way I have described. If you work on your own, I suggest you use an ordinary kitchen timer to keep track of the intervals. If you work with other people then you will need a quieter method of time-keeping. Remember, if you want to get the advantage of the end-effect it is important to stop once the time is up. If you don't keep accurate time then you will tend to lose concentration.

4 The following day you can just continue from where you got to, setting new targets where applicable. Or alternatively you can start again from scratch. I generally prefer to keep going, provided I still have momentum. If I stop work one evening and then start again first thing the next morning, I carry straight on. But if I have a meeting all morning which interrupts my flow of work I find it best to start again with the length of

the bursts all set back to five minutes. Find out what suits you best and then stick with it.

A problem which I am often asked about is what to do with all the papers which are being worked on. Since the rotation system involves working on everything at once, this needs a bit of good organisation.

The simplest solution is to buy yourself some large plastic envelopes or poly bags, say 375 × 250 mm. If you punch holes in the margins you can keep them in a lever arch file. Have one envelope for each subject you are working on and you can quickly gather all your papers together, put them in the envelope and then they are kept together so you can lay your hands on them immediately when you return to the subject. Another method, which takes up a bit more room, is to have a series of stacking trays, one for each subject. Whatever method you use it is important to clear out the envelopes or trays regularly to make sure no documents get stuck there. Don't let them build up!

Let us have a look at how the system we have just been describing fits the criteria for a successful system that we discussed in the previous chapter.

Sufficient regular focused attention

The rotation of work projects and routines ensures that everything we are doing receives adequate attention, *provided* that we have ensured that we have only taken on projects that we have enough time to do. The system also builds in the end-effect so that we work in a focused way.

Resistance and procrastination

Because we are working in short bursts which increase as we build up momentum, it is easy to overcome resistance.

A system for dealing with every piece of work

The method encourages us to deal methodically with everything that faces us. By the use of checklists we can ensure that everything gets dealt with.

Overcoming interruptions and emergencies

When an interruption or emergency occurs we simply deal with it, then return to where we had got to. Similarly, the system is excellent for filling gaps of a few minutes which previously were wasted time because it seemed as if it were not worth starting anything.

So by constructing a simple system on the basis of the principles we have discussed in this chapter, we can achieve everything that we want to. But it is important that we fine-tune this system to suit our own preferences and ways of working, and in the next chapter we will look at several alternatives that you can use to help you to produce your own system.

Action points

- Overcome resistance by initially working for a short burst.
- Remember: the best antidote to fear is action.
- Take advantage of the end-effect by working for timed periods.
- Your mind craves completion – so stopping dead at the end of a timed period makes it easier for you to get going again.
- Take short timed rest periods in which you allow your attention to freewheel.
- Solve problems in your life by writing about them as a stream of consciousness for a timed period.
- Increase the length of timed period you use as you get better at overcoming resistance.
- Divide your work up into projects and categories and rotate systematically round them.

- Use a checklist for each project you are working on.
- Keep your working papers organised by putting them into plastic envelopes in a lever arch file.

Interlude – A Leisurely Sunday

Using the rotation method, it is possible to do the most amazing amount of work in one day if one keeps going, even if there are a considerable number of interruptions. When I was planning my first time-management seminar, I kept a record of what I did during one day and used it to advertise the seminar. Here is a copy of the e-mail that I sent to my mailing list:

Subj: **A Leisurely Sunday**
From: MarkForster@aol.com

Here is what I achieved yesterday using my Time-Management system:
– sorted out my Personal Information Manager (no loose ends left);
– sorted out my audio tape collection;
– wrote thirty hand-written letters;
– revised and printed out my diary for the year and faxed it to my secretary;

– spent forty-five minutes revising the Coaching Book synopsis and printed it out;
– learned twenty words of French vocabulary;
– revised two hundred words of French, Spanish, New Testament Greek and Chinese vocabulary;
– did the washing up twice;
– actioned all outstanding e-mail (no loose ends left);
– tidied my desk;
– actioned all outstanding voicemail (no loose ends left);
– actioned all outstanding paperwork (no loose ends left);
– commenced major sort out of my bureau;
– watched *Vanity Fair* on TV.

Oh, and I did two presentations, one in the morning and one in the afternoon . . . involving being away from home for eight hours.
If you want to be able to work without resistance or procrastination so that you feel totally on top of your work without stress and pressure, then book in for my Time-Management Seminar.

Best wishes,
Mark

8

Variations on the System

The system given in the last chapter is just one way out of many that the principles I have outlined can be used to give us the results that we want. As I said when I outlined the system, you should regard the details rather like the default settings on a computer program which you can adjust to fit your own preferred way of working.

In this chapter I am going to show you some of the ways that you can make these adjustments and indicate what their various advantages and disadvantages are. I would recommend you to try out several until you find the one that suits you best. But it is important to remember that these methods have a training effect and will improve your ability to overcome resistance and work in a concentrated fashion. The result may well be that you find that you outgrow your original system and can move on to something which may have been too difficult for you at first.

I personally have used all of the variants in this chapter and have found that as I progressed so I have preferred a longer burst and to work on fewer items at a time. You may find the same, or may find you react in an entirely different way. The important thing is that the system which you are using keeps pace with your abilities at the time.

First variation – experiment with reducing the burst interval gradually when you finish an item

In the example system given in the last chapter, I recommended that once you had finished as much as you wanted to do for each item, you should restart it at a five-minute burst, e.g.

e-mail	5	~~10~~	~~15~~	~~20~~	5

So in this example you finish dealing with your e-mail during the twenty-minute burst, and on the next pass you start again with a five-minute burst available.

An alternative to this is that instead of reducing to a five-minute burst, you reduce the available burst by five minutes, e.g.

e-mail	5	~~10~~	~~15~~	~~20~~	15

So every time you do not finish by the end of a burst, you *increase* the burst by five minutes for the next pass, and every time you do finish (or have nothing to do) during a burst, you *decrease* the next burst by five minutes.

The advantage of doing it this way is that each of your items will tend to find its own appropriate length of burst. A heavy task like dealing with e-mail or writing a book will end up with long bursts, while something short like tidying your desk-top will probably stay at bursts of five or ten minutes. This means that you naturally end up spending an appropriate amount of time on each subject. This can work well provided that you have built up enough ability to overcome resistance so that you don't need to start off a new series of actions with a five-minute burst.

A variation of this is, instead of decreasing the burst, to maintain it at the same length for one pass before reducing it on the next. The example above would then look like this:

e-mail	5	~~10~~	~~15~~	~~20~~	20

If the work was again finished within the twenty minutes available then the next burst would be reduced to fifteen minutes.

This variation has the effect of stabilising the length of the bursts so that they more accurately reflect the amount of time that you are actually spending on each subject. The time needed will vary from day to day but this method prevents too quick an adjustment. After you have worked with this for a day or so, you will have a very flexible instrument indeed.

Second variation – experiment with varying the length of burst to suit you

You might also experiment with what length of burst suits you best. I recommended a series of 5, 10, 15, 20 etc. because I have found that this is the best way of building up momentum for those people who have serious problems with getting themselves moving. However, what they almost always find is that working in this way greatly increases their ability to deal with resistance, with the result that this series tends to become rather slow moving for them. So when this happens I recommend that they experiment with different ways of increasing the series, such as doubling the length of burst each time, i.e. 5, 10, 20, 40. If this is still too slow moving, then try leaving out the five-minute burst altogether and making the series 10, 20, 40.

Different people will have different preferences and these may develop over time, so do not be afraid of experimenting with what suits you best.

Third variation – experiment with working with only a small number of items

Another method which some people find works more easily for them is to work only on a small number of the items on your list at one time. One way of doing this is to start off with two items and then add one more item at each pass.

To illustrate this, you might start with E-mail and Letters thus:

e-mail	5
letters	5

Once you have done the five-minute burst on both items you would then add another item, thus:

e-mail	5	10
letters	5	10
phone	5	

After you have been working on the list for a while it would look something like this:

e-mail	5	10	15	20	25
letters	5	10			
phone		5	10		
filing			5	10	15
tidy				5	
accounts					5
client follow up					
prospecting					
publicity					
new premises					
letters					
phone					
tidy					

In this example each time an item is finished it is re-entered at the bottom of the list so that a continuous rotation is created.

The advantage of this method is that you are only working on a few subjects at a time and once you have started a subject you quite quickly finish it. The main disadvantage is that you lose the sense of progressing on all your work at once. So this is another method which is best used when you have already succeeded in getting some order into your life.

Fourth variation – experiment with using a standard burst length

When you have gained some experience in using these methods you may well find that you no longer need to increase the lengths of bursts to build momentum, but can use a standard length of burst for everything. I personally find that a twenty-minute burst suits me best if I am using this method. But I would suggest that you experiment until you find the length that suits you – and of course recognise that it may change over time.

Fifth variation – experiment with dividing up an overall time

A method which I sometimes use very effectively and with which you might like to experiment is to have a fixed time for one complete pass through your items, which you divide by the number of items still unfinished. For example if you had twenty items on your list you would start with giving each item five minutes, totalling 100 minutes. If you then finished five of those items you would have fifteen items for the next pass and could allocate seven minutes to each (100 minutes divided by fifteen items, rounded to the nearest minute). By the time you had got down to three items, you would be allocating them thirty-three minutes each and so on.

I have used this method with great effectiveness when I have a large number of items to get through. In fact it is probably the best method of all for dealing with a really big quantity of work. But it is essential if you use this method that you keep at it until you have finished the target you have set for every item. The effect of this method is that the small items get dealt with quite quickly while your attention gets more and more fixed on the larger items.

This method has the advantage of keeping each pass to a maximum length of time. One of the problems of using a rotating list is that it can take a long time to get back to each item if you have a lot of work, especially if it is behindhand, and having a maximum length for each pass helps to obviate this. Of course if this is a continuing problem, the reason is probably that you are trying to do too much. The remedy is to prune your commitments as advised in the earlier chapters. The chapter on structuring your work (Chapter 10) will also help with this as we will be looking at how to arrange your work so that you do not have too many items at any one time.

Case History: Terence

Terence came on one of my seminars early one December and wrote afterwards:

> I've now given Mark's time-management system a week (five days). I adapted it to fit my preferred way of working as he recommends, and here's what I've accomplished so far (on top of all the things I would've done anyway!):
>
> 1 cleared out my desk drawer and filed my important papers (first time ever!);
> 2 moved forward on my taxes (on track to finish by next Friday);
> 3 cleared up the attic room;
> 4 written several pages of a sitcom and a short story (first time I've written in close to a year!);

5   done all the Christmas shopping (unheard of before the 23rd);

6   caught up on e-mails (and started reading my new e-mails again, instead of just filing them for later);

7   passed a test and moved on to the next section in my commodities course;

8   worked a full schedule, including a magazine interview, three new coaching clients, and a day of doing voice-overs;

9   begun sending out Christmas cards (my wife nearly fainted!);

10 spent loads of time with my kids, including going to my son's Christmas concert;

11 watched all the week's football on TV (and done all the ironing!);

12 been to the movies twice and out to dinner with my wife.

I am neither tired nor stressed out, although I am in a slight state of shock!

OK – so what method do I personally use?

The method I use depends on how I am feeling and how well I am overcoming resistance at any particular time. It is important to realise that our moods do not remain the same and we need to fit our methods to how we are feeling.

When I am feeling on top of the world, I probably will not be using any of the above methods but will live according to the 'Beyond Techniques' section of this book. Although this is the natural way of living for some people, it certainly is not for me – so when I am not at my best I find it necessary to give myself structure by using some of the techniques I have been discussing in this chapter and the previous one.

The method I most frequently use (and the one I am using as I write this sentence) is the one described at the end of the First Variation above.

But if I am feeling a bit more confident I find a very effective method is to use a standard interval of twenty minutes, and work on five items at once, replacing each one with a new item as I finish it.

Action points

- Experiment with different methods until you find one to fit you.
- Allow for the fact that you will get better at dealing with resistance the more you use these methods.
- Different methods may fit different moods and circumstances.
- If these methods do not work, the reason may well be that you are trying to do too much. The remedy is to prune your commitments!

Interlude – How Was Your Day?

Here is another example of an e-mail that I used to publicise one of my time-management seminars.

Very unusually yesterday I had a completely clear day with no appointments in my diary. So I decided to see just how much work I could achieve during one full day using my time-management techniques.

So here's what I did from hour to hour throughout the day:

8–9 a.m.
enveloped publicity pack for mailing
wrote and sent out seminar publicity for my e-mailing list
wrote text for newsletter to my network marketing down-line
made bed
tidied office
checked voice mail

9–10 a.m.
cut hedge
prepared OHP acetates for presentation next Tuesday
studied the anatomy of the shoulder joint
read news summary in French from Liberation.com
revised fifty-three items of foreign language vocabulary
etc.
washed up breakfast

10–11 a.m.
checked e-mail
sorted papers for action
rang secretary re missing figures for brochure
purged e-mailing list of undeliverable addresses
planned information for book publication
e-mailed my publisher

11–12 noon
DTP'd my booklet on the Landfill Tax Environmental
Scheme
missing figures faxed from secretary – still some missing!
phoned secretary again
finished preparing publicity pack for mailing
finally missing figures arrived!
rang Kingston Chamber of Commerce re seminar
listed e-mail addresses of attendees at previous seminars

12–1 p.m.
phone call from my wife – re RAC windfall (is my father
still a member??)
finished text for network marketing newsletter
lunch

1–2 p.m.
lunch continues!
tidied office
checked voice mail
studied anatomy of upper arm
listed unknown vocabulary from French newsletter

2–3 p.m.
prepared biographical details for publisher
prepared selling points for book
wrote blurb for book
phone call from Judy C
sorted personal papers
sorted coaching papers
revised 104 items of foreign vocabulary etc.

3–4 p.m.
washed up lunch
checked e-mail – three replies to seminar mailshot already
checked campaign brochure – faxed amendments to
secretary
paid photocopying invoice
sorted out disks
approved new writing paper
phone call from Kingston Chamber of Commerce –
arranged dates
read summary of Church Commissioners' Annual Report

4–5 p.m.
tea break!

5–6 p.m.
tea break continues!
personal details for publisher

6–7 p.m.
prepared artwork for Landfill Tax booklet
e-mailed seminar attendees re case studies for book
supper

7–8 p.m.
washed up supper
DTP'd network marketing newsletter
tidied office
learned sixty new French words

8–9 p.m.
finished publicity details and book description
reconciled credit card statement – paid it
read network marketing publicity materials from up-line
finished selling points for book
revised 133 items of foreign language vocabulary etc.
watched TV

9 p.m. onwards
checked and replied to e-mails
prepared seminar leaflets for posting
watched TV
wrote this summary of the day
sent it out
went to bed!

If your day didn't go quite as well as this, then you need to attend my time-management seminar. E-mail me for details.

Best wishes,
Mark

Mark Forster
MarkForster@aol.com

9

Dealing with Projects

I have mentioned several times that the key to good life-management is to be able to focus our attention in the most effective manner. If our attention is badly directed, all the time-management techniques in the world will not improve our lives, apart from possibly getting rid of some of the clutter. But for real change, we must be capable of directing our focus in an effective way on what we are trying to achieve.

This is not intended to be a book on either project-management or creativity. But because the absence of either makes time-management techniques pointless, I want to give some suggestions for those people who find difficulty with either or both of them. The more capable you are of thinking through a project or a problem deeply, the more likely you are to handle it effectively.

The techniques I am about to describe share a common basis. They are methods of focusing on the whole of a subject by looking at every detail of it. The first is a very versatile tool called 'halving'.

Halving is a powerful technique for sorting out projects

I have already talked about the advantages of making a checklist for a specific project, and how the fuller it is the more effective it will be.

This is a different approach: a checklist that is done one step at a time. I call it 'halving' because it consists of taking everything you have to do and dividing it into half over and over again until you have only one thing left – then you do it.

An example will make this clear. Let's say that you have just decided to start your own network marketing business. You have signed on with a company specialising in nutritional products. It's important you get this business moving as quickly as possible so you want to be thorough in your approach to it. There seem to be an immense number of things you need to do at this stage and the whole project seems a bit daunting. So you decide to use the 'halving' method to work methodically through the action you need to take now.

The first step is to find a category which describes about half the work that needs to be done. It doesn't have to be exactly half, but the idea is to find something which divides all the work into two good-sized chunks. In this example you decide that about half the work that needs to be done is to familiarise yourself with the business. So you write down 'Business Familiarisation' as your first heading.

Now do exactly the same thing to 'Business Familiarisation'. Find something that represents about half the work that needs to be done under that heading. You decide that getting to know the products would fit the bill. So your next heading is 'Product Familiarisation'. About half of that consists of reading the product leaflets and the descriptions of the products. So 'Read Product Leaflets' is your next heading. You could break this down further if you wanted to but you would probably just go ahead and read the leaflets.

So each time you write a heading down it represents

approximately half the previous heading. It's easiest to write them down as a list like this:

Network Marketing
Business Familiarisation
Product Familiarisation
Read Product Leaflets

Remember this is a checklist for action to be taken *now*. You would have a very different list in a week or a month's time.

When you've finished reading the leaflets, cross that item out:

Network Marketing
Business Familiarisation
Product Familiarisation
~~Read Product Leaflets~~

The 'live' heading is always the last item on the list that has not been crossed out. So we are back to 'Product Familiarisation'. Think what else needs to be done under that heading. You decide you need to try out some products. So enter 'Order Products' at the bottom of the list:

Network Marketing
Business Familiarisation
Product Familiarisation
~~Read Product Leaflets~~
Order Products

You may break this down further if you wish, but you will probably just submit an order. When you have done that, cross out the item:

Network Marketing
Business Familiarisation
Product Familiarisation

~~Read Product Leaflets~~
~~Order Products~~

You decide there is nothing further you can do at the moment under 'Product Familiarisation', so you cross that heading off and the 'live' heading then becomes 'Business Familiarisation':

Network Marketing
Business Familiarisation
~~Product Familiarisation~~
~~Read Product Leaflets~~
~~Order Products~~

The next thing you feel you need to do under 'Business Familiarisation' is to study the compensation plan (the system by which you get commission):

Network Marketing
Business Familiarisation
~~Product Familiarisation~~
~~Read Product Leaflets~~
~~Order Products~~
Compensation Plan

We will leave the example there. You should have grasped the idea by now. Note how the system allows you to break actions down until they are as small as you want (or need) them to be – it is usually best to break them down until you arrive at something that you can do with only minimum resistance. The system forces you to work through all aspects of the project one step at a time.

This system can be used in innumerable different ways. The example I have given is of generating a list of *current* actions. But you can also use it to generate *future* actions, such as planning a project from scratch to cover all the action that needs to be taken at any stage. In this case you wouldn't be taking action on each item as you went along but instead would be developing a hierarchical structure on paper. To do this, you need to use indents (which can later become headings if you need to write up your plan). Here is our previous example in indented format:

Network Marketing
    Business Familiarisation
        Product Familiarisation
            Read Product Leaflets
            Order Products
        Compensation Plan

As well as planning, you can use this method as the basis of reports, book outlines – indeed anything which lends itself to being arranged in a hierarchical structure.

Halving can also be used to sort out physical objects

It is not just ideas or actions that 'halving' can be used for. It can also be used to great effect to arrange physical objects. By using it you can sort out your filing system, or arrange the books in your bookshelves – or even sort out the contents of your tool shed, cellar or attic.

I recently completely reorganised my filing system by using this method. Step one was to empty the contents of all my files into a huge heap on the floor. Then I went right through the papers, sorting them into two piles. The one on my left side I called 'Work'. I didn't give a name to the other pile, but it contained every bit of paper that did not come under the heading 'Work'. So you could call it 'Everything Else' if you liked. When I had completed this, I had two piles of approximately equal size.

Then I took the 'Work' pile and divided it into two piles – one pile consisting of my resources work for the church and one for 'everything else'. It is important to distinguish the new 'Everything Else' pile from the previous 'Everything Else' pile, so I made sure that they were kept a few inches apart. When I have a small enough amount of paper to put one pile on top of the previous one, I use a brightly coloured bit of paper to act as a marker between them.

I kept on repeating this process, getting smaller and smaller piles each time, until I had a pile consisting of just one bit of paper. I then decided whether to file that piece of paper or throw it away. I decided to file it, so put it in a new folder. I then continued working on the piles, adding papers to the folder or throwing them away. I started a new folder whenever I felt it was appropriate to do so.

Sorting papers in this way means that the structure of the files happens automatically as you sort the papers. As you go along all the papers get naturally grouped together in context, which makes it easy to see which are redundant, which are duplicates and which are out of date.

If we had been sorting paperwork relating to our previous example of the network marketing business, we might have ended up with the following files:

Network Marketing/Familiarisation/Products/Leaflets
Network Marketing/ Familiarisation /Products/Orders
Network Marketing/ Familiarisation /Compensation Plan

Labelling the files in this way means that all your papers are arranged in a logical order in which it is easy to find the document you are looking for.

My next project was to sort out the books in my bookshelves. Once again I made a huge pile and started by dividing them into Non-Fiction and 'everything else'. I then continued to subdivide them, and every time I got down to one book I placed it on the shelf. Then the next book went alongside it and so on. By allowing the books to fall into the logical order which 'halving' provides, I can now lay my hands on any book simply by thinking where in the structure it would fall.

'Halving' is a very versatile tool. You may be able to think up even more uses for it.

Andrew

Andrew came to me with a problem that is familiar to many of us. He didn't see why he should pay an accountant a large fee to prepare his tax return when he was perfectly capable of doing it himself. Yet every year he had the same problem – he found that he hated doing the job so much that he invariably filed his return late. With the introduction of automatic penalties this was becoming a serious matter.

After I had introduced him to the technique of halving, he realised that this was an ideal method for tackling his tax return. That year for the first time ever he succeeded in producing it on time and with a minimum of stress. 'I used the halving method to make my taxes, an annual pain in the neck, into a totally manageable set of simple decisions and tasks.'

Working on your business is every bit as important as working at it

An important distinction is between working *on* your business and working *at* your business. It doesn't matter whether you work for someone else or work for yourself, or even if your work is paid or unpaid. The distinction is still important.

Working *at* your business is dealing with all the numerous day-to-day details that arrive simply as a result of being in that business. It includes dealing with clients, making the product, keeping accounts, managing staff – in other words *doing* what your business is about.

Working *on* your business on the other hand is more a matter of *thinking* what your business is about. It is looking at where your business is going, refining the vision, setting the goals, dreaming up new initiatives, writing the plans.

The problem we often have is that we get so bogged down in the details of working *at* our business that we rarely spend time working *on* our business. But both are essential for success. It is obvious that there is no point thinking about our business if we never do anything about it. But it is perhaps not quite so obvious that there is little point in working away at our business if we never give thought to where it is going. Yet lack of this kind of strategic vision is a major cause of failure to develop a business. It is the reason why people get stuck in dead-end jobs, why businesses get left behind by the times, why stagnation sets in.

So it is essential that we build into our lives time to think. Real thinking is something that we humans are very bad at because it needs a fair amount of dedicated, uninterrupted time. We very seldom make time just to sit down and think. The very expression 'make time' shows that we think of it as something extra to the 'real work' we are doing. Thinking needs to be done regularly because good thinking is not done in a vacuum. It needs to engage with the real world in action. So the process must be THINK → ACT → THINK → ACT and so on if we want to see progress.

I have many times emphasised in this book that good life-management is not about processing items or work more efficiently. It is about directing our attention in the most effective way possible. And spending time thinking is one of the most essential parts of directing our attention.

As I have said earlier, this is not a book about creativity as such. There are many books that can help you if you want to explore techniques of thinking through and around challenges and problems. But to my mind the most important thing is not whether you use this or that technique, but whether you do it on a regular basis or indeed at all.

Exercise

Here is one simple technique – in fact it would be difficult to get simpler – which you can use as a regular thinking practice.

Give yourself a set time in which you sit down with a notepad and pencil. Make sure you are free from all distractions. Calm your mind and sit quietly and relaxed. All you have to do is write down any ideas or insights that come into your head. Don't worry if nothing comes for a while.

At the end of the time period spend a few moments evaluating what you have written. Make a note of anything that requires action.

The amount of time spent on this exercise and its frequency can vary. An hour once a week or so can produce enormous dividends. Fifteen minutes once a day can keep your ideas fresh and flowing. Remember any thinking time is better than no thinking time.

Whatever length of time you use it is important to keep going for the whole of the time you have set yourself. This is because some of the best ideas often come to us near the end of the period – another example of the end-effect in action. I often find that, once my initial flow of ideas has dried up, I get a second wind which contains deeper ideas and more original ideas than came to me initially.

Another way of working on a project is to use the halving technique to work systematically through every aspect of the project. In this way you can ensure that you have paid attention to everything that needs to be dealt with.

You may be asking how you would fit this sort of thinking activity into your schedule. As it needs a definite amount of time, it is best handled as a depth activity. So the best way of dealing with it is to programme the time into your diary as an appointment with yourself. Don't forget to select a time when you are most likely to do it, such as first thing in the morning.

Action points

- Use the halving method in order to:
  - work systematically through the current action needed on a project;
  - plan future action on a project;
  - sort out your filing system;
  - arrange the books in your bookshelves;
  - clear out your toolshed, cellar or attic.
- Distinguish between working *at* your business and working *on* your business.
- Ground your thinking by using the sequence THINK → ACT → THINK → ACT.
- Set aside regular thinking time.

10

Structuring Your Work

I have already said something about how much easier good systems can make our work, and I want to spend some time now looking at this very important subject in more detail. Closely allied with this is the question of structuring our time to maximise our use of it. When we have a structure imposed on us, we find it much easier to concentrate without being distracted. When we are in the situation of not having anyone imposing a structure on us, then it is important to design one for ourselves.

One of the best investments of your time is to establish good systems

How many times have you been unable to put your hands on some important correspondence because your filing system is not up to scratch? Or failed to follow up on a client because you do not have a clear system for doing so? How many times have you been annoyed by firms that do not reply to correspondence or fail to deliver on promises that have been made? The reason is the same in all cases. Something keeps going wrong, but no one has taken the time and effort to put the system right.

In any job – whether it is dealing with multi-million pound projects or feeding the baby – spending time to set up a workable system will pay huge dividends. Do you wonder why your correspondence always ends up in a pile of unactioned papers? It is because you do not have a system for dealing with it. Do you wonder why you cannot keep up with your e-mail? It is because you don't have a system for dealing with it. Do you wonder why you are always having to waste time popping out to the shops to buy something you have run out of? It's because . . . well, you've got the picture by now!

The good news is that virtually any recurring problem can be solved by working out a system to deal with it. If you are setting up a new project or a new business it is absolutely imperative to get your systems straight. But we are strangely reluctant to do this. We don't have to look far for the reason. It takes less time and effort to make a special journey to the shop for that bit of forgotten shopping than to work out and implement an efficient system for doing all your shopping once a week or so. Especially if going down to the shop provides an excellent excuse for not getting on with work you are trying to avoid.

So, if anything in your life is not working, spend time analysing the problem. Take the process to pieces and discover where it is going wrong. Usually you will have no difficulty clearly identifying where the problem lies once you have taken the trouble to look.

To give a very simple example, I used to have a problem with dealing with the papers arising from evening meetings. In my work with churches, usually the only time I can get together with representatives of parishes is in the evening. So I am often out at evening meetings three or four nights a week. My problem used to be that when I came back from a meeting at 10.30 or 11 p.m. the last thing I wanted to do was any more work. So I had a tendency to throw my briefcase into a corner and forget about it.

The trouble was that I would then continue to forget about it until I needed it again – when I would simply stuff in the papers I needed for the next meeting and go off with it. So my briefcase became a sort of mobile pile of unactioned papers. I usually only got round to emptying it out when I could no longer stuff any more papers into it. By that time of course it would take a major effort to clear all the papers – and like all major efforts it tended to get avoided even further.

When I finally decided to deal with this problem once and for all, I simply went through what was happening step by step and identified that the crucial point was the moment I arrived home. The whole problem stemmed from the fact that I was throwing the briefcase into a corner. Once I had identified that, the solution was easy. I made a rule that whenever I arrived home I would empty the contents of my briefcase into my in-tray. I didn't have to do anything further with the papers that night, but the fact that they were now in my in-tray instead of my briefcase meant that they would automatically get actioned the next morning.

It hardly took me any longer to do than my previous action, but the problem – which had been dogging me for years – vanished.

This is a very simple example. But most systems and routines relating to everyday life and work are not much more difficult to set up. Once one takes the time to look at them, the solution is usually fairly obvious. The whole process of finding a solution boils down to three steps:

1 examine what is happening;
2 identify the exact point at which things go wrong;
3 put it right!

Even in the most complicated problem the only difference is that there will be more than one point at which things are going wrong. Sometimes you can find these straight away. Sometimes it is only when you put one thing right that the other problems become identifiable. So we need one more stage in our process:

1 examine what is happening;
2 identify the exact point at which things are going wrong;
3 put it right!
4 is it working all right now? If not, go back to step 1.

This sort of analytical approach is much more effective than doing what most of us do, i.e. sitting around moaning that we are such disorganised people. If something is always going wrong, tackle it!

Sally

Sally worked in a team of financial advisers. She enjoyed her job, but there was one detail that irritated her. She kept getting clients allocated to her regardless of her own specialities or the amount of work that she already had. The result was that she felt that the other advisers were not pulling their weight. But from the remarks they made, it was obvious that they felt the same about her. This was a constant source of underlying friction in what was otherwise a happy and friendly team.

I encouraged her to follow the process of taking on board new clients from beginning to end. What immediately became apparent was that clients were allocated on an almost random basis. It was usually the person who picked up the phone when the client first called who took subsequent responsibility for him or her. Once she had seen this, Sally was able to go to her colleagues with some proposals for a better method, by which clients would be custom-fitted to the advisers. Since her colleagues all suffered from the same problem, they were receptive to what she was suggesting and the new system was adopted by general agreement. As a result the problem was reduced to such an extent that it was no longer an irritation.

Good preparation is the key to avoiding lateness

I want to spend a little time discussing one specific example of how a systematic look at a problem can go a long way towards solving it. The particular problem I want to look at is one we have mentioned before, which affects many people – that of being constantly late for appointments.

We are all late occasionally – life is never quite predictable enough to ensure that some mishap will not occur to throw off our plans. But we will all have experienced for ourselves the fact that the world seems to be divided into two sorts of people: those who are habitually on time and those who are habitually late. It seems to have little to do with how busy they are – it is a mental clock that has somehow got set late. We know that if we arrange to meet a certain friend at 8 o'clock, then he will turn up at 8.20. If we had arranged to meet him at 8.20, he would turn up at 8.40.

Lateness is a very stressful activity and also very damaging. It can wreak havoc with our work and with our personal lives. It gives a bad first impression and a reputation for always being late suggests unreliability in other things – whether that is justified or not.

If you have a problem with lateness, then applying the analytical approach to it can help. Think of the last time you were late for something – if you are a real sufferer you won't have to think back too far. Try and identify the point at which you first became conscious you were going to be late. Usually that is the point at which you said 'My God, is that the time?' What were you doing at that moment? Most of the time the answer will be the same. You were doing *something else* other than getting ready for your appointment.

The key to avoiding lateness is to identify what time you need to stop working on the *something elses* and turn your attention to getting to your appointment. To do this, work back from your appointment and identify this key moment. I call it the SWEET (Stop Working on Everything Else Time). As I write this passage it is 11.20 a.m. on a bright, sunny morning in early October. This evening I have to travel to a meeting with some clients which starts at 8 p.m. The meeting is taking place in a village some thirty miles away in the depths of the Sussex countryside. So let us apply this process to ensure that I arrive on time.

It's important that I am not late for the meeting, but there's no advantage in arriving particularly early. So I aim to arrive five minutes beforehand at 7.55. I'm not quite sure of the exact location of the house in which the meeting is taking place, so although I have directions I decide to allow ten minutes to find it – 7.45. The journey will take about forty minutes – 7.05. I will need to change clothes before leaving, say fifteen minutes. So the SWEET – the crucial moment when I need to Stop Working on Everything Else – comes at 6.50. That is the point where it is decided whether I am going to be on time or late. If you are a habitually late person, the SWEET is where you need to focus your attention. If you carry on doing other things beyond that point the chances are you are going to be late.

You may have noticed that while I am working out the SWEET, I am not including anything in my calculations about preparing my papers for the meeting or revising the points I need to raise. That is because that sort of preparatory work needs to be done well in advance. I gathered my papers together for the meeting earlier this morning when there was no rush. So all I have to do is pick up my briefcase as I leave, making a quick check that everything is inside. The most common item I used to forget to take with me was my diary; so now I have a simple mental checklist I run through as a routine before leaving.

Developing simple routines is a very effective way of systematising your work. Remember: the better your systems, the more you are freed up to be creative. Simple, easy-to-remember checklists can save time and stop you forgetting important items. When I am giving a presentation, I always remember I have four items to travel with: briefcase; overhead projector; screen and cable. When I want to give my office a quick tidy during the day, I have developed another checklist of four items: books; files;

stationery; papers – even when my office is at its most untidy that checklist will restore order in a matter of minutes. I sometimes used to leave my coat behind at meetings, so I have developed a routine of always putting my car keys in the pocket of my coat so it is impossible to leave without remembering it.

There is nothing special about these routines – they are just examples of how a little thought can greatly ease some of the common problems that afflict us during the average day.

If you work for yourself or at home – or even if you don't – it is important to set up good structures

Many of the people I coach have their own businesses – sometimes in conjunction with employment. Being self-employed is a big challenge because we have to provide our own supporting structures. No longer is there an employer to turn to – everything has to be organised by ourselves. Everything is our responsibility and if we do not fulfil that responsibility then we are the ones who suffer. The big danger is that, because we don't have someone to impose a structure on our work, our work becomes structureless.

My literary agent, Lisa, tells me the story of a recurring dream she used to have when she left the firm of agents she was working for in order to set up her own business. She would find herself walking the streets of a large, impersonal city with no idea where to go because she had no map. She remembers the panicky feeling that accompanied the dream.

When we work within any sort of structured environment it is as if we have a map to show us a large part of what we are supposed to do. Have you ever noticed, for instance, how much longer the day seems when you attend a conference? When we are working at our desks, the day seems to pass in a flash and sometimes we wonder if we have succeeded in doing anything at all during it. But at a conference we seem to cover the most amazing amount of ground in a day. The reason is that a conference usually has a highly structured timetable which ensures that certain subjects are dealt with at certain times.

People who work at home, whether they work for themselves or for an employer, are away from the structure that an office imposes and their work often suffers. Typically there is a confusion between work and personal items with the result that both suffer.

If you find yourself in this situation, the best way to impose some sort of order on yourself is to take a step outside yourself and act as your own boss. Pretend that you are your own employer and lay down the sort of working conditions that you would give a real employee. What are your work hours? How many breaks are you allowed? How much holiday are you allowed to take? Write these conditions down and be as vigilant at enforcing them as a real employer would be.

As a self-employed person or person working from home it is very important to be clear about when you are working and when you are not. That doesn't mean you should not work long hours when it is really necessary to do so. But you must always be clear about the divide. The most effective people I have known at work have also been those who have taken care of their leisure and personal time, even under the most exacting circumstances.

Exercise

If you are self-employed or work from home, take a little time now to set out your own conditions of work. Even if you are employed and work in an office you can still use the same exercise to work out when you are going to do your own personal administration at home. Pretend you are employing yourself as your own personal secretary. What hours are you expected to work? What jobs are you expected to do and how?

Employing yourself gives you a degree of detachment from your work

This principle of acting as your own employer can be extended further. Have you ever been asked by a friend to help them on some aspect of their work? And have you noticed how much easier it is to do their work than it is to do your own? It is rather like the way that it is much easier to give good advice to someone else than to take it oneself. In fact one of the standard questions I use when coaching someone is 'What advice would you give to someone who came to you with the same problem?'

I have often been called in to help friends and colleagues with their bookkeeping. It has proved easy to sort things out for them – but usually at the very same time my own accounts have been languishing at home untouched. My daughter used to be employed as a cleaner while earning money to go to university. She did this job quickly and efficiently – unlike the state of her own bedroom which was knee-deep in chaos.

So you can employ yourself in specific jobs as a way of distancing yourself from your work and giving it structure. For instance, how about employing yourself as your own accountant or bookkeeper? Have a couple of afternoons a week in which you come in and work on your own accounts as if you were working for another person. This standing back from your life and looking at it as if through the eyes of a third party can greatly increase your efficiency.

While you are acting as your own bookkeeper you can draw up a special list of tasks that are exclusive for that 'employment'. Ask yourself: 'If I were working for someone else, what tasks would I be doing?' Confine yourself to those tasks and then you can concentrate exclusively on that area of work.

Of course you don't have to be self-employed or working at home to use this principle. In an office setting you can just as easily set aside a specific time during the week for an aspect or aspects of your work. For instance you might have a day every week set aside for administrative tasks or an afternoon every month for planning. The principle remains the same. During the time you have set aside, you work exclusively at that area of work as if you were someone who had been brought in specially from outside to do it.

Exercise

Identify an area of your work which tends to be a bit neglected. It may be a supporting task like accounts or administration, or it may be a more creative task like forward planning. Decide to employ yourself as your bookkeeper, planner, publicist or whatever. You can even give yourself a grand title to go with the job – such as Director of Finance. Next set your hours of work. What do they need to be? A whole day or one afternoon a week? One day a month? Or what? Schedule these times in and make them as sacrosanct as if you really were going to work for someone else.

You may be able to find ways in which you can reinforce this – perhaps by working from a different desk, or even a different building. When working as my own accountant I take all the books down to the local public library where I am completely undisturbed and even my mobile phone has to be turned off. Or you might try dressing like an accountant, or how you imagine an accountant would dress. It does not matter so much what particular method you choose, as long as you give yourself the feeling that you are working for someone else.

Action summary

- Whenever you have a recurring problem, take time to analyse it and set up a system that works.
- To ensure you are on time for appointments, identify the Stop Working on Everything Else Time (the SWEET).
- Set your conditions of work as if you were your own employer.

- Employ yourself part-time to carry out some of your supporting tasks, such as your own administrator, bookkeeper, publicist and so on.

Interlude – A Fairy Story Revisited

Once upon a time in an alternative universe a merchant's son fell in love with a beautiful princess. Even in alternative universes merchants' sons in fairy stories always seem to be called Hans.

Just like our previous Hans, this Hans had found himself so busy that he didn't have time to deal with all his business affairs and court the princess too. So in despair, he remembered that in the village lived a powerful wizard who was reputed to know everything that was to be known. So Hans went to the wizard's weekend cottage (which was in fact the biggest house in the village) and told the wizard his problem.

'Easy, my son,' said the wizard. 'Chuck everything out of your life that you haven't got time to do properly. Come back when you've done that and I'll give you some more advice.'

So Hans went home, reduced his product lines, hired a personal assistant, resigned from most of his committees, put off learning Brobdingnagian until after he had succeeded in getting married to the princess, and decided to visit her twice a week instead of every day. This of course made his visits much more valuable to the princess and his courtship went better and better. His business prospered too as he had cut out most of the unprofitable lines. Nevertheless one day while he was on his way to visit the princess, his horse went lame because he hadn't got round to getting a loose shoe fixed. The next day he got a bad blister because he hadn't got round to getting his boots mended either.

Since everything else was going so well, these were only minor annoyances – but nevertheless he felt he could have done better. So he remembered the words of the wizard and went back to see him – this time deep in the woods at the head office of his forestry business.

'If it needs doing, it must be done!' said the wizard. 'The small details are just as necessary as the things that seem important. You must ensure that you deal with every area of your work in turn. Rotate your attention!' The wizard then invited him to come again for more advice once he'd put this into practice.

So Hans went home and divided his work up into areas and made sure that he looked at each in turn. He soon had his horse re-shod, his boots repaired, his accounts in order, his parents written to, a new shaving mirror bought, his guttering seen to and his debtors chased up. Best of all he managed to write to the princess every day on which he didn't visit her without its cutting into his other work.

But he couldn't help noticing that some aspects of his life were still causing him problems. His staff kept forgetting to lock the shop up properly so there had been several thefts. A letter from a big supplier had got lost.

Another merchant had developed a more efficient ordering system so was cutting costs. And Hans was sure they should be doing something about this new invention called printing that everyone was talking about – but he didn't know what.

So Hans went to visit the wizard again – this time at his mining operation in the foothills.

'Systems!' said the wizard. 'That's the secret – if something isn't working take the time to figure out why, then change the system so it does work. The time you invest into putting the system right will be repaid a hundred times.'

Again Hans went home and started putting the wizard's advice into practice. He made checklists for his staff to use when shutting up shop, started a booking-in system for incoming and outgoing mail, went through his ordering system in detail to see where it was inefficient, and finally spent an hour a day for a whole week thinking about how to take advantage of the new technology. As a result he was able to flood the kingdom with low-cost printed advertisements which brought back all the custom they had lost to the other merchant and considerably more besides.

With all his new efficiency, things were going really well for Hans's business. But his success meant that his life was getting increasingly fragmented. He never seemed to be able to call a moment his own. He felt that he was being spread thinner and thinner. It was time to see the wizard again.

This time the wizard invited him and the princess together up to his mountain chalet, which had a panoramic view over the beautiful woods and lakes of their native land. There they were able to relax together with their host.

'You need depth activities,' said the wizard. 'Schedule time for yourself on a daily basis. Remember that time you spend with yourself is the most valuable of all time.'

So when Hans and the princess had returned to the plain, Hans started to schedule time to go walking in the woods that surrounded the village. He also made time to meditate every day. He found that he felt less strung out and the days seemed more ordered and easier to cope with. He was also considerably more relaxed, which perhaps the princess noticed even more than he did.

However one thing continued to bother him. And that was that he seldom took time off for a proper lunch and usually worked on late into the evening. He felt that he ought to be able to get his work done in less time than he was. He decided to go and ask the wizard's advice again.

However when he went to the offices of Wizard Enterprises Inc. he found that the wizard was away. Apparently he had gone on an expedition to the desert which lay on the other side of the mountains to prospect for a strange liquid that had just been discovered that you could use to burn to make heat or light or that could be used to lubricate machinery. However, the wizard had set up a chain of post horses to carry letters and other documents between him and his offices, so Hans was able to send him a long letter describing his problem. The wizard's answer came back within a few days and was characteristically concise. 'Employ yourself' was all it said.

Hans puzzled over the message, until suddenly he realised that all his employees had fixed working times and outside those times they went home and forgot about the business. So he sat down and worked out the same sort of conditions of employment for himself that his own workers had. He found that having a cut-off time for lunch and an end-time each day increased his concentration and he got more done. He also decided to employ himself as his own Director of Planning, who worked one day every two weeks. This had a great effect on his business, and it wasn't long before he was able to buy new premises and take on more staff.

It was at this stage that Hans felt he was ready to ask the princess to marry him. She accepted with alacrity. He was after all the richest man in the kingdom by now, apart from the wizard himself.

Coming back from the castle with his heart full of joy, Hans saw the wizard coming along the road in a strange-looking carriage which had no horse. He was obviously back from his prospecting, and by the look of it had found yet another use for the newly discovered liquid. The wizard asked Hans why he looked so happy and when he heard about the princess offered his congratulations.

'I owe it all to you and your advice,' said Hans.

'Well, I have kept the most important bit of advice till last,' said the wizard. 'Whenever you sense that you are resisting something, treat that as a signpost to where you should be going.'

Hans took this advice to heart like all the other advice of the wizard. And as, from now on, instead of avoiding difficulties he tackled them head on as soon as they presented themselves, he and the princess lived happily and productively ever after.

Part Three

Beyond Techniques

Ed elli a me: Questa montagna è tale
   che sempre al cominciar di sotto è grave;
   e quant'om più va sù, e men fa male.

And he said to me: 'This mountain is such
   that when you start at the bottom it's hard work,
   but it hurts less and less the higher you go.'

(Dante, *Purgatorio* IV, 88–90)

11

Resistance: The Signpost to Where You Should Be Going

If you have worked through the exercises so far and have put the systems into practice, you will have learned many things:

- you will have learned what it feels like to overcome resistance;
- you will have learned what it feels like to work in a concentrated manner;
- you will have learned what it feels like to take on only what you can do properly;
- you will have learned what it feels like to progress a project by giving it sufficient regular focused attention;
- you will have learned what it feels like to work within supporting structures;

- you will have learned what it feels like to act on decisions rather than impulse.

I have given you a number of varied techniques to help you get so far, but after you have experienced what it feels like to work in this way for a while you will very likely start to find that you no longer need the techniques all the time. What may happen is that you start to find that, even when you are not consciously using the techniques, you are more able to recognise and overcome resistance, work in a concentrated and focused manner and reject time-wasting activities.

Once you have reached this stage you are ready to consider starting to make the transition beyond these techniques to a state of freedom where good use of time is something you just naturally do.

This final section of this book will help you in making this transition.

We put up resistance to things that challenge us

The key to having control of our lives is knowing how to make use of our feelings of resistance. If we can use resistance positively we will live challenging, exciting and fulfilling lives. If we cannot, then we will be frustrated, out of control, and either highly stressed or a passive 'couch potato'.

We feel resistance to doing something when it is more difficult or more unpleasant than something we are doing or which we could be doing instead. Our natural reaction tends to be to do the thing that provides the least resistance. In the days when the choices in front of people tended to be 'work' or 'starve', this was no doubt a good survival mechanism since the idea of 'work' provided less resistance than the idea of 'starve'. But in our present affluent societies we are so insulated from immediate consequences of this sort that this natural tendency to follow the path of least resistance is no longer appropriate.

We need to be able to distinguish between resistance or fear that is based on real danger as opposed to resistance caused by something that is more challenging or more effortful. We resist driving on the wrong side of the road or grasping live electric wires because we know very well what the consequences are likely to be. But by and large we don't have too much difficulty in identifying when resistance is appropriate and then acting accordingly. What we find more difficult is identifying when our actions are based on inappropriate resistance.

Feeling resistance is usually a sign that you should be doing something

The type of resistance that I am going to be dealing with in this section is the resistance we feel to doing what we know within ourselves we should be doing. Most of the time we know in our heart of hearts what we should be doing – if we didn't we would not be resisting it. We know we should take more exercise; we know we should pay more attention to our children; we know we should get on with writing our thesis; we know we should be following up clients; we know we should do something about the safety report that has just landed on our desk. We feel resistance and we put off taking action. So we end up having a heart attack; our children won't talk to us; we never complete our PhD; our clients go elsewhere; and our firm gets sued for negligence.

These are not things that we feel we should do because they are wished on us by other people. These are all things that we *want* ourselves. We want good health; we want to relate well to our children; we want our PhD; we want our business to be a success; and we do not want other people's deaths or injuries on our conscience. It is the immediate effort that is the problem. The fact that we want something seems to be no defence to resisting the activity needed to achieve it.

In all these cases if we had taken our resistance as a signal to *take* action instead of *avoid* it, the dire consequences would have been prevented. So let us start making resistance our friend and see where it will lead us.

At present in my life the most consistently high-resistance activity I am engaged in is writing this book. Anyone who has ever written a book knows how extremely difficult it is to keep going. The term 'writer's block' is proverbial – with good reason. But by treating my resistance as a friend, as a pointer to the action I need to be taking, I have consistently managed to write almost every day in spite of all the other calls on my attention. There have been days when the writing has flowed and there have been days when every word has been sheer torture, but I have learned that the important thing is just to sit down and do it – however I feel. In this connection, we will now return to something we discussed much earlier in this book.

How are you getting on with the mental strength training?

I hope that while you have been reading this book, you have been consistently practising the exercise that I set you on p. 2. That exercise is designed to get you used to acting as a result of decisions that you have made. This is in contrast to the way that most people act – in a series of impulses which may have very little to do with what they would consciously acknowledge to be their aims in life. The distinction between acting as a result of a conscious decision and acting as the result of an impulse is fundamental to achievement in life. When I use the word 'achievement', I am making no judgements as to what should constitute achievement for you. The whole point is that you are consciously *deciding* what you want to achieve for yourself, instead of acting on a mishmash of impulses which have never been consciously examined.

Acting on our decisions is largely a matter of practice. We get better at it the more we do it. Which is why this exercise is so important. If you have not been doing it regularly, then I strongly advise you to start it. If you started it but stopped, then start again – it gets easier the more times you try it.

The secret to good life-management is to do what we are resisting the most at any one time

If you remember what I said earlier in this book, we have a tendency to take on work as an avoidance measure. But if we tackle what we are resisting first then we no longer need the avoidance activities. We will find therefore that 'busy work' tends to wither away naturally. As we no longer need it to avoid what we are resisting, the temptation to take on more and more is greatly reduced.

So what we are beginning to do now is to make resistance the guide in our life. My earlier analogy of the difference between a river and a swamp comes in here. You will remember how I said that the difference between a river and a swamp is that a river has banks and is going somewhere. What we are doing is making resistance into the banks. Whenever we feel resistance increasing we take steps to reduce that resistance.

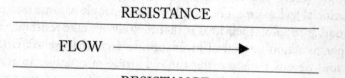

How we do that is all important. In the past we have tried to reduce resistance by avoiding doing what we are resisting. The problem is this doesn't work. Avoiding doing something we are resisting does not get rid of the resistance, it *increases* it. We then get into a vicious circle where we need more and more avoidance activities to avoid feeling the resistance that our avoidance activities increased in the first place.

There are in fact only two ways of getting rid of resistance. They are:

- do what we are resisting, OR
- make a conscious decision not to do it.

The second is important because if we examine why we are resisting doing something we may find it is because subconsciously we know that we would really be better off not doing it. For example, there may be strong pressures on us from other people to do something and our resistance is telling us that we need to grasp the nettle and stand up to them.

In fact there is no real difference between these two ways of getting rid of resistance because what we are really resisting in the second case is taking the decision to examine our true feelings about the situation.

I will be giving you exercises in this chapter which are designed to strengthen your ability, first, to identify what you are resisting and, second, to act immediately to reduce that resistance by doing what you are resisting. They are intended to give you experience of the feel of doing this.

But they are only exercises. The aim is finally to get you to the point where you are capable of doing this naturally without artificial techniques. The simple secret of people who are naturally good at running their lives is that they always take resistance as a spur to action instead of avoidance. In fact what we are talking about here is rediscovering the old virtue of courage. In reality only one thing stands between me as I am and me as I want to be – and that is fear. And the best and only remedy for fear is, and always has been, action.

In order to assist you in making the transition from having to use systems and techniques to doing what needs to be done when it needs to be done, I am going to give you four exercises. Each exercise covers a different aspect of this transition. They are intended to help you as follows:

1 to become consciously aware of when you are acting on impulse and when you are acting on decisions;
2 to experience the difference made by doing things in order of resistance;
3 to become more aware of what you are resisting in your life;
4 to focus on each of the main areas of resistance in your life.

These exercises are best done on a regular basis until you feel you need them no longer. But remember what I said earlier – that our ability to manage our lives fluctuates from time to time, often from day to day. Don't be surprised if there are times when you need to go back and start practising them again.

Exercise 1: Becoming aware of when you are acting on impulse

At one time or another just about everybody has said about some purchase they have made: 'I bought that on impulse.' When that happens it means that we have become aware that we have acted irrationally. We may then try to rationalise the purchase by saying something like: 'Well, I needed it anyway.' But for a few moments at least we have acknowledged that we didn't act because of a conscious intention but as the result of an unconscious impulse.

What we may remain completely unaware of is that, far from this being an occasional aberration, we are reacting unconsciously to thousands of impulses throughout the day. For many people, virtually everything they do is the result of impulse rather than conscious choice. All of us probably act on impulse far more than we would be willing to admit – even to ourselves.

It is important, then, that we become aware of the extent to which we act on impulse. To achieve this we will do an exercise in labelling.

Do this exercise at first for a short period of time, say five or

153

ten minutes. As you get more used to it you can lengthen the time period.

Start the exercise by commencing work on something that you have made a conscious decision to do. It doesn't matter what it is – the essential thing is that you have decided what it is going to be before you start work on it. State your intention to yourself immediately prior to starting work. The best way to do this is simply to say: 'I am going to . . . .now.' So for example it might be 'I am going to answer my e-mail now', 'I am going to tidy my office now' or 'I am going to prepare for my evening class now.' Then start working on it.

As you work, monitor your mind for impulses. These will come at you in various forms, but will usually sound something like this:

- 'I could really do with a cup of coffee.'
- 'I forgot to ring Donald.'
- 'That pot plant needs watering.'

The next thing you know you find yourself making a cup of coffee, or ringing Donald, or watering the pot plant, while your chosen task is abandoned. This seems to have happened without any conscious volition on your part. Indeed that is exactly what has happened. You have not made a conscious choice to do any of these things – you have simply reacted to an impulse.

To short-circuit this process, we will use a method known as 'labelling'. As soon as we become aware of an impulse coming into our mind, we acknowledge it by saying the word 'impulse' to ourselves. Labelling the thought as an impulse in this way brings it into the conscious mind and it is then much easier to let it go and continue with what we are supposed to be doing.

One of the times we are most vulnerable to an impulse getting control of us is after an interruption. So if your chosen task is answering your e-mail, return to the task after an interruption by saying 'I am answering my e-mail' to yourself before any other thoughts have a chance to get in.

Don't try to do this exercise for too long at the beginning. Do it for a short period of time with a definite limit, and gradually extend it as you get better at it. I recommend that you repeat this exercise daily, incorporating it into your normal work, and increase the time until you can do about thirty minutes. Just as a physical exercise session strengthens your body and you get the benefit of this during the remainder of your day when you are not exercising, so this exercise will strengthen your ability to resist impulses and you will reap the benefit in everything you do throughout the day.

Exercise 2: Using resistance to order your day

Earlier in this book I discussed the often heard time-management advice that you should start your day by doing the thing that you feared the most. I pointed out that this could lead to problems of paralysis if we simply couldn't bring ourselves to do whatever it was that we were most fearing.

I also made the point that there is a practical difference between what we fear the most and what we resist the most. We may fear making a call to an irate customer, but what we are resisting is putting right what made the customer irate in the first place.

Although they are certainly closely related, anxiety experienced as resistance tends to be less immediate and more fundamental than anxiety experienced as fear. So it actually makes more sense to rephrase the advice as 'start by doing what you are *resisting* the most'.

If you have worked through the previous exercises in this book, you should now be in a far better position to experiment with this advice. If I had given it to you at an earlier stage, you probably would not be experienced enough in handling resistance to be able to make this advice work.

When most of us are working we have a natural tendency to do the easy jobs first and leave the more difficult ones until later. 'Later', like tomorrow, has a habit of never coming. When this is combined with our other tendency to accumulate trivia as an avoiding tactic, it is not surprising that we find ourselves continually immersed in minor items with the result that we 'can never find the time' to deal with what really matters. The purpose of this exercise is to get you to experience the opposite – what happens when the difficult jobs get done first.

This exercise is basically very easy. Make a list of everything you have to do. Use the halving technique to group items in the order you feel resistance to them. Then start dealing with the highest resistance items and work down to the lowest resistance items.

To illustrate how this works I shall use a list of eight items which can neatly be divided into two until it gets down to a single item. Your list will almost certainly be longer and probably won't work out neatly as a power of two. This does not matter – you only need to divide approximately by half at each stage.

First step – write out your list of tasks:

e-mail
insert new ads
ring Roger
sales figures
contact clients
tidy desk
find missing file
draft report

Second step – tick the items that you feel the greatest resistance to doing. Aim to tick about half the items in total:

e-mail
insert new ads   ✓
ring Roger
sales figures   ✓
contact clients   ✓

tidy desk
find missing file
draft report ✓

Now start a second column and again tick the highest resistance items out of the ones you have already ticked:

e-mail
insert new ads ✓
ring Roger
sales figures ✓
contact clients ✓ ✓
tidy desk
find missing file
draft report ✓ ✓

In this example you have two items in the second column. The next step is to start a third column and tick the highest resistance item again:

e-mail
insert new ads ✓
ring Roger
sales figures ✓
contact clients ✓ ✓ ✓
tidy desk
find missing file
draft report ✓ ✓

Now you have got down to only one item in the column, the next step is to do it. So the first item in this example is to follow up your clients – something which normally you would probably have put off until you had done most of the other easier things. Note that the highest resistance item is often the one that gets the real job done. In this case it is following up clients, not tidying your desk, that actually brings the money in. In the same way my highest resistance item at the moment is writing this book.

You have completed your day's target for following up your clients; so you breathe a sigh of relief and cross the item off the list.

e-mail
insert new ads   ✓
ring Roger
sales figures   ✓
~~contact clients~~   ✓   ✓   ✓
tidy desk
find missing file
draft report   ✓   ✓

Immediately you see that your next task is the only item remaining in the second column – to draft your report. Our natural tendency is to put things like this off until they become urgent. But doing it this way means that you start tackling it at quite an early stage. It may take several days to draft completely but you will have made a good start today. Once you have done as much work on it as you have set as today's target, cross it off the list and carry it forward to the next day.

e-mail
insert new ads   ✓
ring Roger
sales figures   ✓
~~contact clients~~   ✓   ✓   ✓
tidy desk
find missing file
~~draft report~~   ✓   ✓

You now have two ticked items remaining in the first column, so once again tick the one with the highest resistance.

e-mail
insert new ads ✓ ✓
ring Roger
check sales figures ✓
~~contact clients~~ ✓ ✓ ✓
tidy desk
find missing file
~~draft report~~ ✓ ✓

You are beginning to get into easier territory – placing the ads is a doddle compared to following up your clients. After that your next task is to check the sales figures, which you find quite easy. Then, to finish off, you have some relatively simple tasks which you do not have any significant resistance to doing.

Note what is happening here. Resistance tends to be highest to those tasks which challenge us most. These tend to be the very ones which will take our work forward. By starting where we feel the most resistance and ending where we feel the least, we are like a cyclist on a downward slope throughout our day's work. It gets easier and easier as the day progresses and resistance gets less and less. This is precisely the opposite to the uphill slope that we usually inflict on ourselves, where we start with minor routine jobs and throughout the day our work gets more and more difficult. Resistance builds as we find it more and more impossible to summon up the energy to get round to our more important work.

Exercise 3: Identifying what we are resisting

In the previous exercise you were asked to take action on your work in order of resistance, so that the items you were most resisting came first. But unfortunately we often succeed in burying things which we are resisting so well that we are not consciously aware that we are resisting them. So the purpose of our third exercise is to bring more of what we are resisting into our awareness.

Write at the top of a piece of paper 'Something I am resisting in my life at the moment is . . .' Then underneath write as many endings to the sentence as you can. Don't spend too much time thinking about what to write – the exercise is most effective when you write the endings down as quickly as possible off the top of your head. Aim to write at least six and not more than twelve endings.

A client of mine wrote the following the first time he did this exercise:

doing something about my physical fitness
spending more time with my wife and children
answering Sally's letter
facing up to whether I should still be in this job
getting a full medical check-up
catching up with my filing
deciding where to go on holiday
repairing the garage roof
apologising to John

As you can see, the list is a mixture of 'significant' and 'insignificant' items. This is fine. Don't worry about how important the items are – all that matters is that you are resisting them.

Repeat this exercise every day for at least five days, and then repeat it again regularly. Don't worry about whether the items on previous lists get repeated or not. What you will almost certainly find is that your list changes and develops each day. This is exactly as it should be, because the whole point of the exercise is to bring into your consciousness things which you have been trying to keep out of your consciousness.

Don't feel that you have to take action on all the things that come up during this exercise. The fact that you have become conscious of them will in itself tend to produce action in due course when you are ready for it.

Exercise 4: Looking in detail at something we are resisting

The previous exercise was intended to go wide – to bring into your consciousness as many things that you are resisting as possible. This next exercise is intended to go deep – to look at one thing at a time in more detail.

This exercise is a variation on the burst writing exercise that I gave you on p. 89.

This time the aim is to write for fifteen minutes. Start the writing with 'The thing I am most resisting in my life is . . .' and then continue from there. As before, the idea is to write without stopping. Don't stop to think – don't go back over what you have written – don't worry about punctuation, spelling or grammar. Keep your hand moving. When the fifteen minutes is up, stop dead.

When you have finished, read through what you have written and underline anything you feel is particularly significant – such as a new insight or some action to be taken. Then write down everything you have underlined as a separate list.

When you have done these four exercises for a while, then you can start to experiment with living without techniques. Remember our aim is to be able to do what needs doing when it needs doing. To do this is rather like learning to walk. It is not easy and takes a great deal of practice. So do not get discouraged if you find you are unable to live like this for very long. Do not be afraid to revert when necessary to the earlier techniques I have taught you.

Making a practice of taking the following mental steps will help you:

1 Ask yourself 'What am I resisting at this precise moment?' Usually when you ask this question, you will get quite a clear answer. If you don't, then just select anything that you know you are resisting.

2 State to yourself what it is that you are going to do, i.e. 'I am going to . . . now.'

3 Whenever you become aware that an impulse is taking you away from your stated intention, label it as 'impulse' and return gently to your intention.

So your internal dialogue during the process might go like this:

'What am I resisting most at this precise moment?'

'Doing something about my fitness.'

'I am going to spend the next fifteen minutes deciding what action to take to improve my fitness.'

(A few minutes later) 'I wonder if John has replied to my e-mail yet?'

(Cutting short your instinctive reaction to check your e-mail) 'I am deciding what action to take to improve my fitness.'

Scatter maps help you to integrate your day

A good way to prepare your mind for a day in which you are going to use the resistance principle is a thinking technique which I call a 'scatter map'.

A scatter map is rather like the mind-mapping technique that you may be familiar with, but is different from it in some important respects. Personally I have never found mind maps as useful as they are claimed to be. This, like so many things, may just be an individual preference, because I know some people swear by them. However I prefer a freer and easier technique, and scatter maps fit that bill perfectly.

A scatter map is called that because what you do is scatter your thoughts over a piece of paper and map together any connections that come up.

Unlike a mind map, which uses key words, you use complete sentences. This is because a sentence is an important mechanism for integrating your thoughts. Take for instance two words 'DOG' and 'WHITE'. On their own they are just unrelated concepts.

But the second you join them together in a sentence ('my dog is white' for example) a connection is made between them which integrates the two concepts. The role of language in integrating what is going on in our brains is an important one, and I will be mentioning it again in the section in Chapter 13 on journal writing. Once we have a sentence we can add other concepts: DIRTY, for instance. 'My dog is white, except when he is dirty.' We can introduce feelings, e.g. 'I hate it when my dog gets dirty.'

In scatter maps, unlike mind maps again, we make no attempt to make connections between thoughts until *after* we have put them on the paper. They are usually much more comprehensible to the person who wrote them, and much less comprehensible to anyone else looking at them, than a mind map.

Scatter maps can be used for a whole variety of tasks, including most of those for which mind maps are recommended. But the particular use I am interested in here is preparing your mind for your day's work. If you start your day by throwing onto a piece of paper all your thoughts about what you have to do during the day, you will find that you have 'broken up the ground' and that the work itself will be much easier.

On the next page you will see a scatter map which I did myself to prepare for a day's work. In fact it is the genuine map that I did for today – the day I am writing these words. I haven't edited it in any way at all. You will probably find it fairly incomprehensible (which is how it should be) but it will give you the feel for how to do one of these maps – you can of course develop your own individual methods.

What you should note about it is:

- Most of it is written in complete sentences.
- I started in the middle of the page and scattered thoughts wherever I felt like putting them.
- Whenever I sensed a connection I joined thoughts with arrows.
- I described my feelings about what I had to do – 'I love learning Spanish' – 'and don't forget to clean my boots afterwards, UGH!'

I MUST go for a walk! → and don't forget to clean my boots afterwards – UGH!

Revision needs to be done TODAY and TOMORROW (before leaving)

I've been neglecting getting things tidy

↑

What do we need to do today?

↓

Where is the resistance? → I'm resisting both of these!

My book needs finishing ←

I need to prepare for Edinburgh

IT'S LUNCHTIME!

↓

Pack!
Find books, papers, etc.

Read through
Amend
Put in post

↓

Do a scatter map

↓ THIS ONE!

Fun things to do

↓

I want to read Dante again
↳ and Shakespeare

I love learning Spanish and French?   NON! PAS AUJOURD'HUI

- I didn't worry at all about making sense or being logical.

In the next chapter, I will be giving some examples of real days from my own life in which I have followed the resistance principle, or in some cases failed to follow it.

Action points

- Using resistance as our guide to action will cause our lives to flow properly.
- It takes considerable practice to learn to do what needs doing when it needs doing without the aid of techniques.
- Use scatter maps to 'soften up' the day before you start work.
- Don't get discouraged when you fail – get some more practice in!

12

How the Resistance Principle Works in Practice

In this chapter I am going to show how using the resistance principle works in practice. I am going to do this by keeping a diary of a few days in my life, bringing out the way in which I use resistance in order to give my work direction and purpose. This will be a genuine week, not a fictional one, and therefore will have no pretensions to perfection. I will be showing my mistakes and failures as well as my successes. What these successes and failures will be I don't know because the week hasn't happened yet. It starts in reality the day after I am writing these words. The time now is just after midday on a Sunday. The diary will start on Monday morning.

A time journal is a useful tool for analysing your time

Keeping a time journal for a week or so is a useful method of analysing what you are doing and seeing where the time is going. It needs to be no more than a list of the tasks you do with start times.

09.00   Ring Bob
09.12   Open mail
09.25   Reply to Sue's letter

When an interruption comes, indent it and put in an end time as well, e.g.

09.00   Ring Bob
09.12   Open mail
        09.17   Jim phones – 09.30
09.38   Reply to Sue

Using a time journal like this can quickly help you to spot where your time is going and the effect of such things as interruptions and meetings. It is also useful at the end of a busy week to remind yourself of all the things that you actually did achieve.

This diary will be based on exactly this type of time journal which I will then be expanding so that I can draw out the lessons for you. During the period covered by this journal, I will be working solely by responding to resistance as I feel it. I will not be keeping any form of to-do list, nor will I be prioritising my actions in any way.

There are some important things I need to make progress on during the week or keep up to date:

- The most important of all is the writing of this book.
- I am getting a new network marketing venture under way.
- In my work for the Diocese of Chichester I have campaigns to

carry out, new initiatives to get under way and continuing work of contacting and following up parishes.

- I also manage several e-mail lists, including the main one for life-coaches in the United Kingdom, and write an e-mail newsletter twice a month.
- It would be nice to find time to play as well – though my work is so enjoyable and varied that I don't really make the distinction.

One thing I should point out before I start is that I work from home, which has its own advantages and disadvantages, as we have discussed earlier in this book.

Monday – a day that goes well

One of the great advantages of working at home is that you don't have to get up early to get to work. So I am not out of bed until 8.10 a.m.

One of the great disadvantages of working from home is that it can be very difficult to get going in the morning. Without the necessity to present oneself fully dressed and reasonably awake at a specific time and at a specific place, the tendency is to slop around in a dressing gown while vainly attempting to get some momentum going.

Responding to resistance can cure this very easily. The effort of getting dressed can seem like an insurmountable mountain when you first get out of bed. But just remain alert to what you are resisting right now. That will lead you step by step through the process of getting up until you are ready to face life fully dressed, showered and awake. Doing this day by day will build up a routine which takes very little conscious effort, but will also produce a lot of resistance if you are tempted to neglect it.

So here I am, fully dressed, showered and awake at 8.30 starting breakfast. The post arrives containing a book on the Pilates exercise system which I want to try. At 8.55 I feel resistance beginning to build up to the idea of starting work – a sure sign that it's time to get going. But as I am about to start, the vicar of the parish I am visiting this evening phones with some last-minute arrangements. It is now 9 a.m.

I start my work by asking myself a question I will be continuing to ask myself throughout the day. 'What am I resisting the most at this precise moment?' The answer is obvious to me. At the beginning of a week there is always an accumulation of tasks that have had to be brought forward from the previous week. These are often because someone was unreachable or for other good reasons (time-management experts don't have *bad* reasons for not doing things of course). I keep items that have been brought forward (B/Fs) in a dated accordion file so whenever something needs following up I simply note down when to look at it again. Good follow up is essential for success in almost any sphere of human activity, so if you don't have a system already I advise you strongly to start one. Some people keep B/Fs in their diary, some on their computer. I prefer an accordion file because I can file the letter or other paperwork connected with the item that needs following up. The important thing is that, whatever your system is, it works for you.

B/Fs tend to have big resistance because by definition they are things which have been put off, even if there were good reasons for doing so. So checking my B/F list for the day is my highest resistance item.

Accordingly the first action of my working day is to check my B/F list. When I do so I find that the only item on it is one phone call that I have to make. The phone call itself though is providing less resistance in my mind than something else, so I don't action it straight away. It is 9.09.

The thing that I am resisting more than the phone call is working on this book. I have already completed the first draft and have four and a half months to the delivery date, so what's the hurry? Well, writing a book is a high-resistance activity, and that four and a half months will vanish seemingly overnight if I don't keep working at it. Consistent action is the key to a large task like this. So I work on the book for about forty minutes.

Note that I do this *before* I get immersed in the routine tasks of the day. This is not a deliberate plan – it is simply the result of dealing with the highest resistance items at any particular moment. It is now 9.48.

Now I can turn my attention to the phone call. It is to a vicar I have been trying to get hold of without success for some weeks. My natural tendency is to put off following this up hard enough. The amount of resistance that has built up in me tells me this is the next thing I must tackle. I ring his number and get his answering machine. I leave a message and (very important) put a B/F note in my file for a couple of days' time. It is 9.58.

Today's mail is sitting in an untidy pile looking at me. Like many people I have an aversion to paperwork and so decide this must be the next thing to get on with. In fact, to my relief, apart from the book on the Pilates exercises, there is little more than junk mail and I have dealt with everything by 10.20.

This evening's meeting is beginning to hover like a black cloud so my resistance monitoring tells me that preparing for it is the next thing to deal with. I have to check the exact location and how to get there, and also print out some customised overhead projector slides. This is done quite quickly and I put all the papers in my briefcase. I work out the SWEET ('Stop Working On Everything Else Time') for the meeting as 7.10 p.m.

It is now only 11.12 a.m. and I am already feeling that I have broken the back of the day. I have worked on my book, made an important follow-up phone call, cleared my paperwork and done all the preparation for the evening meeting. It helps of course that I don't have any backlog of work to clear – but that is only because I have been applying the resistance principle consistently to all these things in the past.

The rest of the day will definitely be an easy ride downhill, comprising items I feel comparatively little resistance to. But this is a *danger time* when it is easy to start drifting. So it's very important to keep mentally monitoring resistance levels and avoid impulsive actions.

Now I check my e-mail. One of the e-mail lists I run has received an offensive message from an outsider. I have to deal with this. There are also quite a number of new subscribers to the lists and these need to be processed. And as usual there is a lot of minor correspondence, some of which needs replying to.

It is important to have a good system for dealing with e-mail, especially if you have a high volume. It is very easy to let it get thoroughly disorganised. I usually receive thirty to forty e-mails a day, which is a lot less than some people. Remember: time spent working out a good system is always repaid many times over. The system I have developed for e-mail goes like this:

- First of all I give new e-mails a quick read through, deleting any that I can straight away.
- Then I deal with the remainder in strict order of receipt. My aim is to clear all emails as I receive them.
- I only file e-mails when I have a real need to. Otherwise I delete them.
- Once I have finished reading and replying to them, I then send the replies in one batch.

Usually a few new e-mails have arrived by the time I send the batch. I will glance through them but not action them unless there is something urgent. I leave them until my next major download. This is important because it is quite possible to spend the whole day receiving e-mail, replying to it, receiving some more, replying to that, and so on.

It's now 12.50 and I find I am resisting taking a break. Don't imagine that what we resist are always the hard things. Our resistance varies throughout the day and there come times when it is relaxation and enjoyment that we are resisting. Listen to what your mind is telling you – the better you get at doing this the better balanced your life will become.

I have a light lunch and try some of the exercises in my new book. Having got the major resistance items out of the way, I have now reached the level of minor errands – but it is still essential to keep aiming at where I sense the most resistance. At 2.07 I go out in order to pick up a prescription. I am back at 2.43 and ring the watch-repairers to find out whether my watch is ready. They say they will ring back. So at 2.46 I look through my diary at the week to come. Regular scans forward of your diary are necessary if you are going to be well prepared. I am already well up to date with most things, but realise that there is some information I need to print out about a training day on Saturday for my new network marketing venture.

Halfway through doing this, the watch-repairers phone back to ask me to 'give us another couple of days'. I put a B/F in my file for Friday, and while I am doing it make a note to follow up on Wednesday the tapes I ordered for my second-stage mailshot. I cannot start the first stage until the materials for the second stage are ready as it is essential to make an instant response to any enquiries.

At 2.54 a colleague rings to change the time and place for our meeting tomorrow. We were going to meet at his house at 11.30 a.m.; now he needs to change it to 12 noon at the offices. No problem.

It is now 3.02 and I realise that the non-arrival of the tapes has given me an excuse to put off getting my stage one mailshot ready. I ought to have it ready to start sending out as soon as the tapes arrive. If I don't do this it will mean that when the tapes do finally arrive there will then be further delay while I finish preparing the material.

I spend the next forty minutes addressing envelopes. Once these mailshots are established, this is the sort of task that one can pay someone else to do. But at this experimental stage it is easier to keep control if one does it oneself. At 3.40 I check my e-mail again as I expect my earlier messages about the e-mail list will have stirred up some reaction. They have, but only a few quick replies are needed.

At 4.10 I realise I am still resisting getting all the mailshot materials completed. I make a few small changes to the stage one flyer, print it out and at 4.30 drive into the town centre to get it photocopied. It is going to take some time so I go and buy a few stationery items I need. Shopping centres are dangerous places, full of temptations to goof off, so I make sure I am back at the photocopy shop in good time. I have to wait for another ten minutes but that is better than the time (and money) I would have wasted if I had allowed myself to let my impulses rip in the shops.

I get back home at 5.40 in time to help my wife choose colours for a new sofa and then I go for a brisk walk at 5.50 for fifteen minutes before relaxing over a book for half an hour before our evening meal. The voice of resistance is telling me here that it is time to relax.

At 7.15 I leave for the evening meeting. As we have seen, I prepared everything for it earlier in the day so there is no last-minute rush. I have checked how to get there so I do not waste time getting lost. Everything goes smoothly and I get home at 10.40.

Arriving back from an evening meeting is another *danger point*. I spend a few minutes sorting papers out, rather than immediately flopping. I know this will pay dividends the next day.

Summary of the day

I have done an enormous amount during this day, and I have hardly wasted any time at all. The great thing about a day like this is that it leaves you feeling energised and alive, rather than exhausted. Working in this way takes a very low toll in terms of stress because stress is discharged by action as soon as it is felt. Flopping, goofing off and procrastinating do not discharge stress but repress it instead, leaving you feeling worse than you did before.

Tuesday – getting back on track after a disaster

Because I was working late last night I make a leisurely start to the day and don't commence work until 10 a.m. After yesterday's activities my office needs tidying. I follow the simple routine I mentioned in an earlier chapter:

books: put all books back on the shelves
files: put all files away in the filing cabinet
stationery: put everything back in its place (my definition of stationery includes everything not contained in the other three categories)
paper: collect all papers together ready to be dealt with

This quick sort takes less than five minutes and leaves me ready for action. I check the answer machine: there is one message – for my daughter.

It is now 10.12 a.m. and the meeting with my colleague at 12 noon is hanging over me. I get the papers ready and work out the SWEET as 11.15. It is now 10.26.

I check my B/Fs from yesterday and ring the vicar I was trying to get hold of. His phone is engaged, so I leave a message on his answer machine and download my e-mail. Just as I am about to start on that, he rings back. He has been away. We finish our business quickly and I continue dealing with my e-mail which fills the gap neatly until it is time to leave for my appointment.

An incoming phone call makes me leave slightly late for the appointment, but I have allowed a small margin for error so this doesn't worry me.

I arrive neatly on time to find my colleague is still tied up in another meeting. I fear the worst when I learn that the meeting started twenty minutes late. In fact it is an hour and ten minutes before he is free from the meeting. I am mentally kicking myself. I have brought no work with me so there is nothing I can get on with. *Lesson One*: always have something constructive to do if you are kept waiting. But, even worse, I realise I should never have agreed to the new time for the meeting in the first place, knowing that it was going to be preceded by something with an indefinite end time. *Lesson Two*: never agree to imprecise appointments.

So at 1.10 we go out to lunch, find a suitable place by 1.30. Sit and talk until 2.45. I drive him back to his office by 3.05, spend a bit of time sorting out a few things with him there, and am back home by 4 p.m.

This is an extremely good illustration of how one short meeting can take up an entire day. Our actual meeting duration was one and a quarter hours. Achieving this took up four and three-quarter hours out of the middle of my day. *Lesson Three*: don't go to meetings at all unless there is a real identifiable need for them.

When a disaster like this occurs (and they will occur sometimes in spite of our best efforts) the really important thing is to get back on track again immediately. If one doesn't, the knock-on effect can last for days.

I arrive back home to find my tapes for the stage two mailshot have arrived. That means I can start sending out the stage one mailshot. I get the first batch ready and catch the last post.

Then I do my learning revision for the day – 210 items, mainly of foreign language vocabulary. By now it is 6.22. I have cleared the two highest resistance items (mailshot and learning) since I got back. This has got me feeling energised again, and I sense that I am over the hump and on the downhill slope again. I can turn my attention to some lower-resistance items, but it is still very important to keep monitoring where resistance lies, otherwise I will just go off into impulse activities. I check my diary for the following day and check the answer machine – there are two messages for action tomorrow. I note them as B/Fs.

At 6.27 I download e-mail again – there are several changes to the subscriptions of the various lists I run. This takes me up to my evening meal at 7.35. During the evening I spend a further hour working on my mail drop.

Summary of the day

There was the disaster of a meeting taking an unexpectedly huge chunk out of the day. Even so I managed to get back on track, and also made sure that I examined what went wrong and learned the lessons from it so that I don't allow myself to be put in the same position again.

Wednesday – progress on all fronts

I start the day off with a scheduled call from a client at 9 a.m. and then write my book until 11 a.m. when I take my daughter to work. I continue writing after that until 12.05 when I get a phone call from the treasurer of one of the parishes that I wrote to on Monday. We arrange a meeting for the following week.

I am becoming conscious that I am resisting acknowledging that my office needs a more thorough sort out than the quick tidies I have been giving it. So I embark on a thorough spring-clean of the office floor which takes me an hour and half, broken only by a phone call from another parish arranging a meeting.

Feeling very virtuous, I snatch a late lunch and am interrupted by a phone call from a television production company that wants to consider using me in a new self-development series. They need me to provide biographical details and say they will fax me more information. There is nothing further I can do about it until I receive the information.

It is now 2.15 and I start work on paper, phone calls and other minor tasks. This occupies me until 5.45. Then I remember I have been putting off returning a book to a friend. I get this ready for the post. I check my e-mail again and deal with one new subscriber. It is now 6.45 and I spend the forty-five minutes until supper revising vocabulary. After supper I do an hour's work on my mailshot in between picking up my daughter from work. Then I write my e-mail newsletter on coaching for an hour and ten minutes until it is time to watch *Ally McBeal* on television. After that is finished, it takes ten minutes to send out the newsletter and then to bed.

Summary of the day

Again a very productive day, in which all the main threads of my life were progressed forward. Although it is a long day, I do not feel tired because this is an energising way of working. As resistance falls, so one's energy level rises and what gets done at the end of the day is positively pleasurable.

Thursday – some bad mistakes but a successful outcome

I have a dentist's appointment at 8.45 and when I get back from it I make a bad mistake and do not start work on the high-resistance tasks immediately. Coming back from a meeting is always a *danger point* and this time I fail to get moving immediately and instead lounge around reading the paper. This of course makes me feel terrible, as purposeless or impulsive behaviour always does.

Finally at 10.37 I summon the energy to get working properly. My biggest resistance is getting the biographical materials written for the television production company, whose fax has now arrived. I have a struggle to get working on this, but succeed in completing it and getting it in the post by 12.43. This makes me feel much better.

My expenses are due today and I always hate doing them, so this is the next item I tackle. I have them finished by 1.05 and have lunch.

I then decide to tackle something a bit less threatening and download my e-mail. There is a huge amount today and rather than tackling the job head on I allow myself to get distracted and sidetracked. The result is that I don't clear all the e-mail until nearly 5 p.m. Even worse than the e-mail having taken so long, I now feel stressed and uncomfortable. This is the result of allowing myself to act in response to impulse rather than overcoming resistance. It is a good lesson in the fact that our feelings of stress come from *not* working through our resistance.

Having got off the right path, the really important thing now is to get back on it, otherwise there can be repercussions that may last for days. Goofing off tends to have a knock-on effect – so once we have recognised what we are doing, our first priority is to break the sequence.

This we do by stopping what we are doing and forcing ourselves to ask ourselves the question 'What am I resisting?' Often it can be quite a struggle even to ask the question. As always, the way to reduce the resistance is to focus on smaller and smaller segments until you arrive at something you can do.

So I know I have been resisting something all afternoon. There was in fact something I was resisting more than dealing with my e-mail – and the trouble I had with the e-mail was directly due to the fact that I shouldn't have started on the e-mail at all while something more threatening was left undone. Doing the e-mail was an escape activity at that moment, even though it wouldn't have been if I had tackled it in its proper place.

So finally I forced myself to ask the question 'What am I resisting?' and the answer came back loud and clear – 'Writing my book'. By now the idea of writing my book had built up a considerable amount of resistance. I realised that I had been pushing it away all day. Even the trouble I had had getting started again after visiting the dentist was due to it.

I was beginning to have that panicky feeling of paralysis that can lead to complete goofing off. However once I had allowed myself to identify the problem, I knew what to do. I simply focused on the feeling and asked myself what the first step in working on the book was – 'opening the file on the word-processor'. 'Could I do that?' – 'Yes!' Immediately I opened the file and found myself typing. The feelings of resistance had entirely disappeared.

There will inevitably be times when we get stuck and the key to getting moving again is the sequence I followed in this example. Isolate the feelings of stuckness, then reduce the feelings by breaking them down into an easy first step:

- 'What am I resisting?'
- 'What is the first step in doing that?'
- 'Could I do that?'

If the answer to the last question is 'No', then break the first step down further until the answer is 'Yes'.

An example will show how this works:

Q. What am I resisting?
A. Calling potential new clients.
Q. What is the first step?
A. Call Client A.
Q. Could I do that?
A. No!
Q. What is the first step to calling Client A?
A. Look up her phone number.
Q. Could I do that?
A. Yes!

Summary

Because I tried to escape doing what I was most resisting, the day was stressful. Most of what I did as escape activities I would have done anyway at some time during the day, so no permanent damage was done. But by doing them in the wrong order I was experiencing stress instead of energy. Had I not faced up to what I was doing in the early evening, this might have ended up causing a large knock-on effect over the next few days.

As it was I got back on course and wrote for an hour or so on the book during the evening, as well as working on my mailshot.

Being prepared to learn lessons from our failures is essential to growth

Because I succeeded in getting back on track on Thursday evening, Friday was another day in which I successfully progressed the important themes in my life. If I had not got back on track on Thursday, I would probably have started Friday off badly.

Often the only way to get back on track if one is experiencing this sort of knock-on effect is to go back temporarily to one of the short-burst rotation sequences.

What you will note from this journal is that whenever something went wrong, I took the trouble to go back and identify exactly *where* and *why* it went wrong. This meant that I was continuously able to improve my performance.

Action points

- A time journal is a good way to spot where time problems lie.
- Have a system for bringing forward items that need to be followed up later.
- Identify your own *danger times* and *places* when you need to be particularly watchful for impulsive actions.
- When something goes wrong, make sure you get back on track at the earliest possible opportunity.
- If you find you are resisting something so much you can't get started on it, then break it down until you can do the first step.

Table 2: The effect of using resistance as a guide

What happens when you use resistance as a guide	What happens most of the rest of the time
What is important gets actioned first	Minor items get actioned first
The day gets easier as it goes on	The day gets harder as it goes on
Anxiety and tension are dispersed	Anxiety and tension build up
Procrastination is eliminated	Procrastination increases
Real work gets done	Busy work gets done
Busy work withers away	Real work is avoided
Concentration is maintained	Distractions abound
Crises are prevented	Frequent crises arise

13

More about Depth Activities

In Chapter 6 I discussed some of the characteristics of what I call 'depth activities.' I defined them as those activities which help us to become more deeply involved in our experience of the present. In that chapter I contrasted them with most of the rest of our activities, which tend these days to have the effect of making our lives more and more shallow at the same time as they spread them wider and wider.

There are of course an immense number and variety of possible depth activities. In this chapter I want to focus on just three of these. The distinguishing feature of these three is that they are not only worth doing in their own right but that they each have a well-attested positive effect on our general effectiveness. Therefore any time that we set aside for them is likely to be well repaid by our increased abilities during the rest of the day. In a sense perhaps I should have made this the first chapter since you could significantly increase your ability to handle your time effectively by just incorporating these three activities into your life, even if you ignored everything else in this book.

Many people of course will already be doing at least one of these activities on a more or less regular basis. You may very well be tackling it in a completely different way from the methods I am going to be recommending. If what you are doing works for you, that is absolutely fine. My advice is intended for those who are trying the activity for the first time, or who have tried and failed to incorporate it into their lives on previous occasions.

The three activities that I will be looking at are:

- walking;
- meditation;
- writing.

Walking is the easiest, best and most pleasant form of exercise

There is plenty of research to show that exercise is good for your health. But an interesting development is that some recent research has shown that it is good for your mind as well. People who exercise regularly have been shown to have increased alertness and effectiveness at work.

This may not come as a great surprise to those who do exercise regularly, because most people who do so report that their day seems to go much better when they exercise and much worse when they fail to. This is true to some extent of any depth activity – it helps to frame the beginning of the day and get us into a relaxed and alert mood. But exercise also increases the general overall efficiency of all our bodily processes. The more efficiently our bodies are working the more efficiently our brains will be working – which are after all a fairly important part of our bodies.

Unfortunately an entire industry has grown up directed at selling us the latest 'essential' equipment we absolutely must have before we can engage in the latest exercise craze. This ranges from videos through designer sportswear, to expensive gadgets and gym subscriptions.

We also seem to have been seduced by the idea of 'fitness' as an end in itself. The average person really does not need to have the physique of a boxer or an athlete. It's fine if you *are* a boxer or an athlete or have ambitions to be one, but frankly to have a toned physique when you are a sedentary office-worker is a bit like owning a four-wheel-drive off-road vehicle, complete with bull bars, which you never use for anything more demanding than taking the children to school and driving to the local shopping mall. It has more to do with conforming to a fashionable image than with the reality of being healthy and effective in one's life. Fitness and health are not necessarily the same thing – as anyone who has suffered a sports injury can testify.

This sort of fashionable pressure does damage because it leads many people to give up on exercise altogether when they find it impossible to conform to the image. They are discouraged from taking the sort of exercise which really would be useful to them – exercise which would increase both their health and their mental sharpness. Unlike the hours of time, large amounts of money and unswerving determination which the fashionable images demand, this type of exercise is both easy and cheap.

In fact the best general exercise is the easiest and cheapest of all – walking. Twenty minutes of brisk walking three times a week has been shown to have just about as much health benefit as any other form of exercise. And it is far less likely to cause injury, either in the short or long term, than most others. Walking is less damaging to the joints than jogging, safer than cycling, more convenient than swimming. If you are a dedicated jogger, cyclist or swimmer, I am not suggesting that you should give up on these activities. But walking is ideal for those who are not taking sufficient exercise at the moment because they have been given a false notion that it has to be difficult and demanding before it does any good.

The other advantage of walking is that it is a natural human activity that gets us out into the open air. This in itself helps us to look at life in a deeper way. If we are stuck in front of a computer screen all day, it will put us back in touch with the rhythm of the seasons, make us experience again what it is like to be beneath the sky, give our body a chance to work at a temperature other than room temperature. Walking is in short a thoroughly pleasant, enjoyable and healthy activity. Which makes it much more likely to be persevered with than other types of exercise.

I only have two bits of advice on setting up a walking exercise programme (you don't need me to tell you how to *walk*, do you?):

- wear suitable footwear;
- start gently and build up gradually.

Meditation is well-attested as improving our effectiveness

There have been numerous studies on the beneficial effects of meditation – ranging from improving general health to increasing the ability of executives to solve problems at work.

Most people who take up meditation seriously will report at least some of the following effects:

- I have a greater sense of calmness.
- It's much easier to relax.
- It makes the day run smoother.
- I find I'm less impulsive now.
- My mind races less.
- My relationships have improved.
- I'm more effective at work.
- I feel more in touch with myself.

Like walking, meditation is basically a very simple, natural and easy human activity. Unfortunately, like exercise, it has been made to seem far more difficult than it really is. It has also collected all sorts of spiritual and religious associations which put some people off and divert others from its essential simplicity. Meditation is not a spiritual practice any more (or less) than sitting quietly on a chair is a spiritual practice. Sitting quietly on a chair in a church with the intention of praying to God *is* a spiritual practice and similarly meditation can be used for spiritual practice for those who wish to do so. But that is no reason why those who do not should be put off it with the result that they never experience the benefits which it can bring.

There are hundreds of different methods of meditation and there are also hundreds of books about meditation, and anyone who wants to cover the subject in more detail will find no shortage of material. But if you are merely interested in increasing your daily effectiveness then the method I am about to give you will produce as good results as any. It is also extremely easy – which makes it the meditation equivalent of walking for exercise.

Most people find that meditation works best if it is done every day, and twenty minutes is the most favoured length of time for a session. Find yourself a quiet spot where you will be free of interruptions. Sit on a firm chair with your spine straight so that you are naturally balanced. Fold your hands in your lap or rest them palm upwards on your thighs.

Now shut your eyes and let yourself relax for a moment or two. Then fix your attention on the sound of your breathing. Whenever you find yourself distracted from the sound of your breathing, bring your attention back to the sound. It doesn't matter how often this happens – just bring your attention back every time you realise that it has strayed.

That's it!

Writing is the most effective method for integrating your mind

Writing is one of the most fascinating of human activities. There have been numerous studies on its effect on such various topics as creativity, psychological health, intelligence and even longevity.

Many of the people we think of as geniuses were prolific writers, whatever their field of endeavour. Edison, Van Gogh and Einstein – to name just three – left an almost unbelievable quantity of written documents. There has even been some suggestion that it was the prolific writing that made them into geniuses, rather than that they wrote prolifically because they were geniuses.

There seems to be evidence that the human brain needs to put ideas, feelings and experiences into language before it can integrate them fully. Writing is one of the best ways to facilitate this process.

I have already given several writing exercises in this book. These have used four different methods:

- free-flow writing;
- writing down ideas during a timed thinking session;
- sentence completion;
- scatter maps.

All of these allow your brain to put its existing connections into language which then makes them more accessible for further connections to be made. All these exercises are therefore progressive. If you repeat any one of them on the same subject for several days you will find your thought develops and changes, sometimes quite dramatically.

The exercises I have given are useful when you need to tackle specific problems, but it is also possible to use writing in a way similar to exercise and meditation – as a systematic regular practice with the aim of improving your general functioning. This is the practice usually known as 'journal-writing'.

There are not quite as many different ways of journal-writing as there are of exercise or meditation, but nevertheless there are quite a few possible variations on the theme. The one I am going to give you is what I have found most effective for myself. This is quite intensive, but very effective.

My method is to use the free-flow writing technique (see p. 89) to write three pages a day on anything that comes into my mind. I use a spiral-bound, lined A4 notebook to write in. This takes me about thirty-five minutes to complete.

I do not set myself any subject to write about, but let the writing take me where it will. However it is important to write both about facts and your feelings about those facts. Writing about facts alone or feelings alone is nothing like as effective.

So if you are writing about a particular problem, as well as describing the problem itself you might write about the feelings of frustration the problem is causing you or your fear that you might not be able to find an answer. Writing about both fact and feeling enables your brain to integrate the two. This practice will greatly increase what has recently become known as your 'emotional intelligence'.

My own experience of writing like this for a period of about eight months, during which I hardly missed a day, was quite incredible. I described it at the time as like having a new brain. My mind became full of ideas, which seemed to bounce off each other. I became much more energetic and problems of procrastination fell away of their own accord. Although for various reasons I now write in my journal far more sporadically, I remain convinced that the practice left me with a permanently raised intelligence and far more self-awareness.

I cannot guarantee of course that this practice will have the same effect on you. But the evidence seems to suggest that most people would benefit enormously from giving it a try.

Incorporating these activities into your life should be a gradual process

My advice to anyone wanting to take up these three activities would be to avoid attempting to start all three at once. That is an almost certain route to failure because you would need to make far too sudden an adjustment to the rest of your life to allow for them. It is much better to select one and get that well established into your life before starting the next one.

You will remember that my advice in Chapter 6 about depth

activities is that each one should be scheduled at a definite time each day so that it is not crowded out by other activities. You need to experiment with what is the best time for each activity so that it is right for you. My own preferences, which could be a good place for you to start, are:

- *Journal writing – immediately on getting up.* I find this is the only time I can do this quite intensive activity. If it is left till later, too much resistance builds up. So I set my alarm clock half an hour early, get up and start writing before I get dressed, make a cup of tea, or do anything else.
- *Walking – lunchtime.* A brisk walk makes the ideal break at lunchtime. It gets you out of the office into the fresh air, and stops you from eating or drinking too much. You will return invigorated, ready for the afternoon's work.
- *Meditation – on finishing work.* Meditating when you finish work provides a good end to the day's activities (remember the end-effect), and also allows you to free yourself of the tension which will have built up. Some people find a better time is just before they go to bed because they find it helps them to get to sleep. This is very much an individual preference.

We are now at the end of this book. If you have put into practice everything that I have written in it, you will have learned far more than just how to get everything done. You will have transformed yourself into a courageous, unstressed, healthy, intelligent and profound individual. I wish you every blessing on your journey.

Action points

- Walking and other types of mild aerobic exercise have a beneficial effect on your mental alertness as well as your physical health.
- Meditation has a proven track record of increasing effectiveness at work as well as helping with relationships and self-awareness.

- Writing is the number one method of increasing your mental effectiveness.
- Introduce these activities into your life gradually, not all at once.

A l'alta fantasia qui mancò possa,
   ma già volgeva il mio disio e'l velle,
   sì come rota ch'igualmente è mossa,

l'amor che move il sole e l'altro stelle.

Here power failed my high imagination
   but already my desire and my will
   were being turned together, like a well-balanced wheel,

by the love which moves the sun and the other stars.

(Dante, *Paradiso* XXXIII, 142–145)

How to Contact the Author

If you are interested in any of the following:

- becoming one of my coaching clients (limited vacancies available);
- arranging a seminar;
- being on my mailing list (seminar dates, further titles, etc.);
- my free monthly e-mail newsletter;

then you can find up-to-date details on my website at www.markforster.net. Alternatively you can contact me direct by telephone on 01403 250016 or by e-mail at MarkForster@aol.com.

Index